TOMMIE
& GROPE

MATT JOHNSTONE

Outskirts Press, Inc.
Denver, Colorado

Tommie and Grope
A Novel
All Rights Reserved
Copyright © 2007 Matt Johnstone
V4.0

Outskirts Press
http://www.outskirtspress.com

ISBN-10: 1-4327-0260-2
ISBN-13: 978- 978-1-4327-0260-1

Outskirts Press and the "OP" logo are trademarks belonging to
Outskirts Press, Inc.

Printed in the United States of America

DEDICATION

This Book is dedicated to
my beloved wife of 34 years
May she Rest in Peace

EPILOGUE

"For the grossly impudent lie always leaves traces behind it, even after it has been nailed down, a fact which is known to all expert liars in this world and to all who conspire together in the art of lying. These people know only too well how to use falsehood for the basest purposes."

-Adolph Hitler

DISCLAIMER

This novel is a work of Fiction. The pathological liars, paranoid schizophrenics, criminals, incompetents and other perverts appearing in this book are a figment of the author's imagination. Any resemblance to real persons living or dead is purely coincidental. Places mentioned in this book are also fictional and the Juvenile laws and the Health and Human Services laws and procedures in the State of New Jersey may be totally different than those represented in this book. The thoughts and opinions in this book are purely those of the author and the Publisher cannot be held responsible in any way for its content. The author retains all copyrights to this novel. Any duplication of the content, except for review and promotional purposes, is prohibited, unless authorized in advance by the Author or Publisher. Furthermore, any individual (i.e., official and legal holder of copyright) that objects to their quotations being included in this novel may request that it be removed from future printings. An official written and signed request sent to the Publisher via fax or regular mail made by the copyright holder and/or their legal representative on company or legal letterhead will be honored.

CAST OF MAIN FICTIONAL CHARACTERS AND LOCATIONS

Uranus – Villain, Pathological Liar, and Paranoid Schizophrenic

Tommie – Victim daughter, Brainwashed Uranus Trainee

Grope – Victim son, Bug Boy, Bionnacle Wizard

Matt Johnstone– Yours truly, fat fingering author

Katie – Hero and Friend

Jack – Katie's Navy husband and supporter of our cause

Cherry – Hero and Friend

Martin – Cherry's Tennis Pro husband

Guido – Villain and Slimy Criminal lawyer

Curly – Kids Biological father

Brady – Curly's live-in partner

Dumpy – Victim Doggie

Nana Anna – Step-on-Mother afraid of her own shadow but caring

Booby – Ignorant and faithful friend of Uranus

Ms Fargo – Grope's Teacher – Special Ed - NOT

Paris Mason – Lawyer that nailed Guido – good for her

Francis Stein – Last CINA CPS Lawyer – Good Lawyer that helped us

Leslie Smart – Curly's Family Lawyer

Judge Dread – Inept Child Court Judge and Guido's buddy

Selma – CPS Social Worker – She cared but rarely followed through

Feather – CPS villain Social Worker puppet of Uranus

Tack – Former Marine and all talk, no action neighbor

Moe – Curly's brother who has fallen on hard times

Tom – Maintenance Manager of the Apartment Complex

Seaford County – a make believe county not too far from New York City

Arrowhead – a make believe town in Seaford County New Jersey

ACKNOWLEDGEMENTS

I would like to thank several individuals. This book would not have been possible without their help. First and foremost, I would like to thank my editor and mentor, Nickie, who spent considerable time straightening me out, ensuring consistency and accuracy within the story. After all, there is always some truth, even in a fictional novel. Next, I would like to thank my courageous friends and relatives for reviewing the book several times: Yawn! The honest comments I received from them, and the continuous encouragement I was given, kept me going during the difficult times. Believe me, there were many trials and tribulations over the year and a half I spent writing the novel. Last, but not least, I would like to thank Lisa for her patience and guidance during the Publishing of this novel.

PROLOGUE

"Insane people are always sure that they are fine. It is only the sane people who are willing to admit that they are crazy"
                                                    - Nora Ephron

Long ago in college, I learned through my studies in Psychology that insanity exists in all of us in a number of ways, and at a number of levels; however, we are usually able to control it. According to Freud's Structural Model, the id, ego, and superego, the id is the part of the psyche that doesn't care about reality, about the needs of anyone else, only its own satisfaction, or is the id a small fresh-water cyprinid fish? Regardless, Tommie and Grope is a story about two young children with a biological mother that is a pathological liar possessing only an id – self gratification or fish – you take your pick.

I do feel deep compassion for a number of special friends I have made over the last year or two. I can say with certainty that the conflict and stress inflicted on all of us involved have been Herculean. The horrors that enveloped us all brought some of us together, and separated others. The initial intent of the novel evolved from simple note taking into chronicling everything that affected our lives, imaginary or not. I made a promise to a very special set of friends to write this story. I did, lightening the darkness through some humor, with hopes of healing some of the wounds. There is always truth hidden within the fiction.

There is much perverted comedy in this story. There is also

sadness, as well. I want to clearly state that there was no direct intent on my part to hurt anyone, especially those that think they may be characterized in the novel. Perhaps this story will enlighten them with the truth. I expect we all know who we are – well most of us anyway. Some of the characters remain in la-la land, and are totally impervious to insult, hearing only what they want to hear, such as the perverted villain in this drama.

This story includes a long drawn out court case concerning blatant child neglect, drawn out because of the many delays planned by the defense, total defiance of orders issued from the court, an ineffective Health and Human Services Organization, a completely negligent County Youth Court system, and one egomaniac criminal attorney who cheated and lied to the court in order to win at any cost.

Mom, as the Seaford County Child Protective Agency calls her, was once a friend until I discovered just whom and what she really is – a controlling pathological liar and schemer, a woman entirely motivated by her quest for self gratification; but I am repeating myself here, and wasting valuable ink and trees.

So friends and readers, find yourself a comfortable place, sit down and relax, and if you are Grope, turn out the lights before reading. Grope's eyes glow in the dark from all the bugs he has eaten, so no light is required for him to see in the dark. Come to think of it, perhaps keeping a small empty bucket nearby your chair would be good too, because some of the text is quite graphic. A comfortable seat in the bathroom comes to mind. Keep the lid down and pad the seat to avoid hemorrhoids.

CHAPTER 1
STREET SIDE

T he story begins on a cold, blustery fall day in our small town of Arrowhead, New Jersey. I had just parked my Explorer across the street from the Maytag apartment complex where I lived. Upon exiting the car, I spotted two women chatting next to the lamp post in front of my one bedroom, first floor apartment. The woman to the left of the pole was a chunky, but not a bad looking blond. I guessed her to be in her mid thirties. The woman to her immediate right was a fairly tall, rail-skinny, pasty faced redhead with a slightly hooked beak of a nose. What made the redhead stand out was fact that she was dressed like a wannabe teenager, more like a hooker. Her pink short shorts were skin tight, and her extra large, bright red sweatshirt had a yellow Semper Fi logo. As I approached them, I heard "fracking this and fracking that" rolling out of the redhead's thin lipped mouth. I thought at first she must be a sailor that had undergone a sex change – without adding boobs. But then I noticed a tampon string hanging out from between her legs, and besides, sailors don't wear Marine Corps sweatshirts – so go figure!

My second vehicle, a coal black Chevy pickup truck, parallel parked directly in front of my corner apartment was blocked by a double-parked, beat up white car with a US Marine Corps sticker in the rear window and an out-of-date license plate that read USMCSLUT. The double parked car obviously belonged to the redhead. Yep! Semper Fi. Broad Assed Marine - not Navy – but that's close enough!

The two ladies, and I use that term quite loosely, checked me out as I approached, about to walk behind my truck and into the building. They appeared to be friendly so I waved to them. They waved me over to them. Now, I have a pretty good sense about people, and I had seen all four of the old Omen movies so I should have realized right then and there to ignore the women and get out of Dodge. But, being widowed for several years and alone in the area, curiosity got the best of me. I simply said hello with a wide toothy grin. I was greeted with very friendly smiles, a hello, and stop and talk to us grins. So for the next thirty minutes, maybe more, Uranus, the pasty faced redhead, spouted out her entire life history. No one could get a word in edgewise. Her words were delivered faster than any Indy race car. Yes, her name is Uranus. I have heard of Venus, the goddess of love and a great tennis player, and Mars, the God of war and a good candy bar. But Uranus – that's a new one to me, other than the planet. Was the name symbolic in any way? I'll leave that up to the reader to decide. Somehow, the name seemed to fit her.

I learned during the non-stop, one sided conversation that Uranus had just been evicted from her apartment nearby because a crazy neighbor bitch of a woman had reported her to the police for child neglect. She prattled on that the charges were totally ridiculous because she had only been gone for a few minutes, with her two underage kids at home alone. She said that she was arrested and spent three days in jail. I learned later that this was not her first arrest, or conviction for that matter. While in jail, her kids were taken away and Fostered with her good and faithful friend Booby. This arrangement had been ordered by Seaford County Child Protective Services. Yep, Booby was the chubby friend that I was looking at, standing there looking bored and saying nothing. She must have heard this story a thousand times, I am sure.

After repeating herself numerous times, the real story began to emerge. The police and Child Protective Services were let into the house by Grope, her twelve year old son. The Social Workers and police smelled smoke from candles that had been blown out before the door was opened. They also found the house to be cold and totally dark. Flashlights illuminated a house filthy to the core, and the children unclean, cold, and unfed. After her return home and arrest, Uranus told the police that she had only been gone for a few minutes to the store to get dinner and there must have been a power failure. The real story came out much later. The utilities, gas and electric, had been shut off due to lack of payment. She had been away from home for several hours. Yes, Uranus had told Social Services and the police that she had been out shopping for groceries, but in truth she was hours away in New York City having carnal knowledge with a Navy Reserve boyfriend; Yep, snack time for her, and cold starvation for the kids. Later, Uranus revealed that her twelve year-old boy child suffers from Obsessive Compulsive Disorder (OCD) and is Autistic with Asperger's Syndrome. The girl child, three years younger, actually looks after the boy much of the time, because mommy dearest liked to play away from home. In truth, the little nine year old daughter performed the duties of a stand-in mom. But, as I said, all this came out later.

Uranus said that a court hearing was to be scheduled soon; actually two hearings would be held; one of them would be a criminal trial and the other a Social Services Neglect Hearing. She said that she had hired a kick-ass criminal attorney, Guido, who told her he could and would get her off completely. Guido was recommended by someone at her church of all places, and he would certainly help her, in part, pro bono. I think I know what that means - Pro boner. I soon learned that Guido is as slimy as wet goose grease and has no morals. In other words, he

3

is a great criminal defense attorney. She was right on that point.

To my total surprise, I discovered that Uranus attends the same church that I do. I also found out that she served during the Gulf war; well, she served in Okinawa because she didn't believe that women belonged in combat areas. She was given the choice while at Camp Pendleton, so she chose Okinawa. While in Okinawa, Uranus received a medical discharge from the Marine Corps. She suffered knee injuries, and, as a result, she qualified to receive a monthly check for life. Hmmm, knee injuries – go figure. I didn't bother to ask her if she also had TMJ. Anyway, at the time, her sad story got my full attention and sympathy. She was very convincing and seemed so sincere. She was definitely in need of help. None of the real truth had emerged yet, only unrecognizable hints. Having close ties with the Military, being a Veteran of the Viet Nam era, and having several relatives in the Navy and Marines, I offered to help her in any way I could. After all, what are good neighbors and Military Family for?

Boy was that the mistake of the century!

So here I am standing at the curb starting to fall asleep from her psycho babble jabber when another new neighbor wandered out of the apartment building portal, walked over, and joined in the conversation. Tack, as he introduced himself, is a former Marine who, as it turns out, has the same MOS as Uranus (a packing specialist - Hmmm) - Semper-Fi again.

"Uranus is moving in upstairs," Booby finally announced. These were her first five words other than hello.

Uranus then announced, "I have no credit, and I am losing my clearance and job at work because of the ridiculous allegations made against me by that crazy bitch."

"To make it worse," she added, "I have to let my former Foster mother Nana Anna move in with me so I can get the apartment." She said, "I really despise my mom. I had to kick her out of my apartment once before because she is such a fracking slob. I will give her another chance though. She deserves that."

These words rolled off her tongue as if she could have rented the apartment without her. You see, Uranus really had no credit, no money, and couldn't even get a checking account because of her bad credit.

I am so damn blind. Uranus is the smoothest talker I have ever met. We were all taken in. "We'll help – yada, yada, yada."

"Hey," said Tack, "we're a military family and need to look out for one another, right?" RIGHT! Other than talk, that was the last help Tack ever gave her. Yep, a smart man, Tack.

As time passed after our first meeting, Uranus often let words flow out of her mouth better left unsaid. For example, she told me in a conversation that all men who offered to help her expected sex from her. She added that her beauty was a real curse. She said that even her co-workers were jealous of her because she got all of the attention from the men in the office. Now don't get me wrong, Uranus is attractive in a strange kind of way; but I could never say she is hot looking. How many rail-skinny, flat-chested, hook nosed forty year old women that dress like teenage hookers are there? Several, I am sure, but not one of them is "hot" looking in my humble opinion.

Uranus said that she trusted me, and she didn't worry about me at all, primarily because I was way too ugly and much too old for her anyway. How subtle is that? To be honest, I wouldn't have touched her with a rubber coated broomstick. But, I was trying to be neighborly and I was sympathetic to her situation, and, therefore, willing to help. But, I am getting ahead of myself.

So the die were cast – **snake eyes**. Moving day was near, and Uranus needed help moving. Could she borrow my pick-up truck and SUV to help in the move? OH YEAH! Could she use my vacuum because hers didn't work very well? OH YEAH! "I'll bring it along and help clean as best I can," resulting in a four hour scrubbing in the shower and throwing out my clothes and the vacuum bag when I got home; but that comes in the next chapter.

CHAPTER 2
MOVING DAY

Well, the big day arrived. I walked out of my apartment into the sunny Saturday afternoon chill (I love to sleep in now that I am retired, well permanently disabled, but that is another story). I saw the monster moving truck parallel parked in front of my apartment stuffed to the gills with Uranus' treasures. Did I say that Uranus was moving to the third floor of my apartment building? So, the truck was in the right place, blocking several other cars, and I wished that I had gone out the other exit. I spotted Uranus's moving helpers as they were busily unloading some strange looking metal and plywood furniture, placing parts on the sidewalk in preparation for porting the material upstairs – all stairs – no elevator here.

After I said hello, one guy in his mid thirties said that he and Uranus were good friends and that he was a Chief in the Naval Reserve. Military – go figure. He had on an old, weathered flight jacket complete with flight crewman wings. I used to have a flight jacket too, until a college girlfriend borrowed the jacket along with my only memento service uniform for a Halloween party no less). I never saw her, the jacket, or uniform again. Maybe she was shanghaied and sent to Viet Nam?

I assumed the Navy guy as nothing more than a social friend of Uranus, because he had a smoldering cigarette dangling out of his mouth as he worked. Uranus had mentioned during our first conversation that she hated smokers. That said, she quietly told me later that he was great in bed but she would never get emotionally involved with him because he smoked, and he refused to quit for her. She elaborated further by saying their sexual sessions were a good stress reliever for her, and he was madly in love with her, so she could use him for sex whenever she wanted. "During those times," she muttered, "I just have to put up with the smoke stink. He is a good lover, but he lives too far away to allow me to see him all the time." I didn't know yet, but this was the guy that Uranus was boinking while her kids sat alone in the cold and dark apartment. I found that out later during one of her rambling midnight confessionals, but more on that later.

Navy boy was accompanied by another young man, smaller, thinner, and a lot younger; perhaps he was his son. We all spoke briefly, told a few sea stories, and I started to help unload the truck onto the curb.

Along the inside perimeter of the truck bed, Uranus or her friends had placed a bunch of old wooden planters and several concrete flower pots. These items were too heavy to cart upstairs, and had no place to go. She sweetly asked me if she could store them on my patio for a short time. Assuming there were only a few, I said OK. Twenty pots and several dilapidated planter boxes later, I was ready to tell her forget it. No lifting for me, so we used a hand cart to port them and I acquired help moving them to my patio. The pots and planters were all filled to the rim with her "special" dirt, whatever that means, and each pot weighed a ton. Well, so much for sitting on my patio people watching. My entire patio was occupied with rows of trashy looking cement, weeds, rotten wood, and dirt. "Temporary" is the operative term here. This junk remained on my patio until just before I moved out a year later.

After the "garden" was unloaded and placed on my patio, Uranus asked me if she could store a few of her "excess" possessions in my storage areas; maybe I offered, I don't remember. You see, I had rented two fairly large storage areas across the street to hold the remains of my furniture and shop tools from my five bedroom house that I sold two years after my wife died. Many of these items were just too difficult to get rid of. Uranus did straighten out my storage areas, having been a "packing specialist" in the USMC and all. She was really good at it but, let's not go there. Uranus proceeded to cram my storage areas full of junk you wouldn't believe: an old rickety plant table made with glued-on broken colored glass fragments that spilled everywhere, an old stained and smelly couch, boxes of plastic do-dads, suitcases, plastic bins and bags of old clothes, tarps, wooden posts so old and rotten they looked petrified, and, of course, more special dirt stuffed into huge plastic containers. Junk was piled to the ten-foot ceiling. Uranus also had some other wood in her apartment that she wanted to use for something exotic, planning to cut up the wood in my tiny garage woodshop at some point in time. She hauled the wood to my garage and it rested there against the side wall until just before I moved out. OH YEAH, she had all but moved in to my apartment.

Long after dark, the truck was finally emptied, swept out, and returned. It was time to drive to her old apartment with my truck and vacuum. Navy boy had to go for the night, because cleaning was not his thing. Uranus, in front of God and everyone, gave Navy boy a sloppy open mouthed sucking tongue kiss on his neck, and whispered something in his ear that made him grin like a Cheshire cat. He walked back to his car stiff legged. Perhaps she spoke of things to come later if you get my drift.

CHAPTER 3
CREEPY CRAWLIES

A short while after the moving truck left, I drove to Uranus' old apartment, directions in hand. The apartment was located on the second floor of a multi-story apartment complex, similar to where I live. The building appeared well kept on the outside, but years older and musty on the inside. I climbed one flight of stairs, walked to her apartment and knocked on the door. Uranus shouted, "Come on in." I opened the door and almost fell over from the stink of urine and pine sol. Uranus had acquired a dog, a Basenji named Dumpy, and she was not house-trained, the dog that is. The inside of the apartment was an abomination, a filthy mess. Cleaning was already underway. After entering, I wondered what the place had looked like before Uranus started moving, when the house was full of the stuff they had taken out of the truck. The very thought sent chills down my spine. How much crap had been thrown out? I shivered at the vision of all the junk on the truck jammed into this apartment, and then shook it off. "Be nice," I told myself. "Be nice."

Entering the living room, I met Uranus' two kids and "Nana Anna," Uranus' former Foster mother. Nana Anna was busily scrubbing the kitchen. The children seemed very friendly, but I could immediately tell that the boy was a bit strange.

I found the boy Grope fairly tall for his age, quite thin, with thick, dark hair, cut into a crew, and dark brown eyes almost hidden by overly thick eyebrows. He seemed extremely withdrawn. Grope carried a huge plastic creature in his left hand that he poked at me saying, "He's going to eat you." Then he reached over and placed his right hand on the crown of Uranus's head and said, "I want to suck out your brains." Honestly, Grope was spooky to the max. After a few minutes, he wandered back into Uranus' bedroom, an area with the lights off, so he could read.

The girl Tommie, on the other hand, appeared bubbly and full of life. I found her to be a pretty child, with dark, shoulder length hair, big brown eyes, and a tiny nose. She was dressed entirely in boy's clothes, a dark blue t-shirt, below-the-knee tan shorts with multiple pockets, and old sneakers. Tommie seemed very mature for her age, probably because of her responsibilities with the boy. Grope was much taller than Tommie, actually a little taller than Uranus, and not much shorter than me. I got the feeling that Grope pestered Tommie a lot and that she tolerated it. Tommie was helping clean; Grope was in his own little world, reading, or sucking out the brains of something, maybe cockroaches or rodents.

Shortly after arriving at the apartment, I met a friend of Uranus'. She came downstairs from her own apartment to help us out. The young woman looked very familiar to me. We both stared at one another for a bit, and it finally dawned on both of us that we did know each other; of all things from Camp Pendleton, California. Her name is Katie. You see, my daughter is a Marine Corps wife. Katie is one of my daughter's former on-base neighbors, and good friend. I had met her on base a few years ago and visited with her and her family a number of times while staying with my daughter. How bizarre is that?

OK! Uranus must be a good person, because Katie is a good friend of both Uranus and my daughter. How's that for illogical logic? Both Katie and I were about to be royally sucked in.

I brought in my Oreck XL vacuum with a fresh bag installed, and began cleaning up the floors and closets. The tile floors and carpet were covered with old dried up food, papers, and other things I didn't want to know what they were. I swear some of the stuff moved. Every wall in the house had been painted with a rainbow of various colors. Many walls were peeling and some were smeared with dark globs, perhaps food or something gross. There was mold in the bathrooms that must have been growing for two years. I would not have been surprised if this had been a former crack house; it was so filthy and run down. The carpets were thread bare in areas, and stained with unimaginable spots: red, blue, green, blood, urine, tea, and other caked on stuff that I didn't want to guess at. As I said, I had put in a new vacuum bag before I left my home for Uranus' apartment, and the bag was half full after cleaning Grope's room – ARRRGHH – YUK.

I repeat; there were many dark smears of something gross on Grope's bedroom walls, many more than in the other rooms. Don't ask what, I didn't get that close. All this mess, and Uranus claimed to be a neat nick – go figure.

I guessed that Uranus would be fined big time for extensive repairs. So did Katie. It turned out that she was fined, and she complained bitterly about it. Personally, I would have torched the apartment, and rebuilt it from scratch. Never had I seen such filth. Well, enough of that for now but remember the look, because it becomes relevant later.

Not too long after I arrived at Uranus' old apartment, the children stated that were hungry and so were the rest of us. I offered to buy, and I left the apartment to pick up pizza for everyone. Having returned to the apartment with pizza and sodas, we all wolfed down the food, and got back to work. Grope ate like a starving animal, smearing food everywhere. Great table manners I thought, but then again, it must have been hard to eat Pizza with a huge bionnacle stuffed in his left paw.

Satiated, Grope wandered off to find a dark spot again to read, suck brains, or do whatever.

It was after midnight when we finished with the apartment. We had filled a dumpster on our way out. I drove home to crash. My truck was loaded with stuff from the house. Hopefully, there weren't any crawly things mixed in because we wouldn't unload until the next day. I didn't want anything growing or nesting in my vehicle. Exiting my truck in the parking lot, I manipulated the vacuum out of the vehicle through the rear hatch, carefully removed the vacuum bag from the vacuum, and threw the bag into the dumpster. Then I turned the vacuum upside down and shook out excess material that had spilled over. A huge dust cloud rose in the night air. Later, I would take the Oreck apart and clean it properly with my shop vac. Upon unlocking and entering my apartment, I stripped down, threw my dirty clothes into the garbage, and stepped into the shower. I proceeded to scrub myself raw with a loofah sponge, hot water, and soap. Skinless, but clean and tired, I flopped into bed. Falling asleep, I wondered to myself, what comes next? It sure didn't take long to find out.

CHAPTER 4
THINGS THAT GO BUMP IN THE NIGHT

Around midnight during the next week, a few days after the move, I heard banging and thudding noises a few flights up from my apartment. The hammering sounds began rattling the entire building. You guessed it. Uranus was busily constructing a jungle scene in her son's bedroom, complete with cargo nets, murals, and camouflaged painted walls. Bugs, birds, snakes, lizards, spiders, plants, stale food, urine, and human feces were yet to be added. Steel poles framed his overhead bunk bed and stained mattress (we won't go there). There was a work and play area underneath his bed to store his collection of bionnacle toy creatures with claws that leave marks on the body. The room already smelled like Cambodia in the seventies. Maybe the special dirt she had placed in my storage area was destined for the floor of the jungle. That would complete the scene.

Directly underneath Uranus and her creepy brood, lived a quiet man that works at the local Army base collecting and processing bodies of soldiers delivered home from the Mid-East war. The noise from above was driving him and his visiting boyfriend insane. After all, it was very late at night, and he needed sleep. The man put on his slippers and robe and stormed upstairs. He banged on Uranus' door to complain about the noise. Answering the door, Uranus was confronted by the man. He was in a deep rage, screaming that the noise was keeping him up, and that his pussycat was suffering from shell shock. He told her to stop the hammering, and whatever else she was doing immediately, or else. Uranus apologized profusely, and said she thought he was not home. Didn't he work night shift? Of course, the rest of the occupants of the apartment building must work the night shift as well. Unsatisfied, he stomped off, swishing down the hall toward the stairs, very upset. Early the next morning, he filed the first of dozens of complaints against his new upstairs neighbor. She and her noisy bunch of animals must go.

Shortly after the incident, the battle between Uranus, pussycat man, and building management began. Daily complaints were being filed, and the "deranged" neighbor, according to Uranus, swore that he would get her thrown out of the building. He was fuming, claiming that he had to pay for a pussycat psychiatrist to de-traumatize his prize pet. He even had to have his boyfriend come by and baby-sit the pussycat while he was out to calm her down. You see Siamese pussycats are very sensitive to disturbances of any kind.

It didn't take long before a hearing was held between the irate neighbor and Uranus, with management mediating. Uranus was asked nicely by the Apartment Manager if she would be willing to change apartments – move to a location where she would not have anyone under her. She flatly refused, claiming that the noise in the apartment was normal, and that the neighbor was over-sensitive and being vindictive.

I was told later that the neighbor had made a bet with his boyfriend; a bet that he could get out of his lease so they could get a place together. This news came from Uranus, but I believed it for some reason. Having been asked by Uranus, Katie and I did listen for noise from her apartment and nothing appeared out of the ordinary, except when Uranus was wrestling with Grope or Dumpy, the doggie, or Grope was jumping from his ceiling bed to the jungle floor in the early morning (THUMP!!). Apparently, the dirt and clothes on his floor didn't muffle the sound. Even Tack and his wife could not hear any noise and they were on the second floor, adjacent to Uranus' apartment. We mentioned our observations to Management, but they did not appreciate the intrusion into what was not our business.

During a discussion one evening, Uranus informed me that Grope had a serious oral fetish and was constantly asking her, Tommie, and Nana Anna if he could suck on their toes. He was persistent. When he did suck on their toes, mom would suck Grope's toes to make him stop. This, of course, had to be noisy. Slurp, Slurp! Gag!

Then she laughed, and told me that I needn't worry. Grope would not want to suck on my toes because he only liked to suck on good looking feet, and my feet were ugly. I thought to myself, "Thank God for ugly feet."

Anyway, everyone hears noises in apartments. For example, my neighbor directly behind me must have a steel bed frame positioned on the back wall of his bedroom, located directly behind my bed. It rhythmically bashed into my wall around two AM about three times a week. The noise didn't last very long, maybe a minute or two, but then neither did the live-in girlfriend. Go figure.

Pussycat man did get out of his lease with no penalty, and Uranus was given written notice from Management that another noise complaint may result in her eviction. Actually, her accusation about the bet turned out to be the truth. Pussycat man had made the bet because wanted a place nearer work. Yep! The ruse worked for him. He bragged about it just as he was moving out. A truth from Uranus – I'm impressed!

Uranus refused to change apartments because she had already decorated and painted her entire apartment with a rainbow of colors. She had hung bamboo curtains and installed a room separator for Nana Anna and Tommie to share the smallest bedroom. She had made jungle scenes for Grope, and installed Eastern art wall hangings in her huge bedroom upstairs on the fourth floor. Besides, it took an entire day to fill her illegal waterbed, and the carpets were already stained with doggie poop and urine. Grope's room already had his poop neatly smeared on his walls, his bed, and the carpet. The kids' rooms were piled knee-high with clean and filthy clothes mixed together on the floor. The bathroom had finally taken on the aroma of a New York subway station urinal. So, the house was cozy and just how she wanted it. There had been too much work already invested in the apartment to make it look like another crack house to move now. Besides, she had not broken in her bed and shower with a real man yet, and the sheets were still somewhat clean.

A month later, a nice Korean couple moved into the apartment below Uranus, replacing pussycat man and no further complaints were filed. Of course, by that time, Uranus had already deserted the children and fled to Iraq, but I am getting ahead of myself here.

CHAPTER 5
HIDE OUT

Actually, hiding out became a regular occurrence once Nana Anna had moved in with Uranus. Unfortunately, her hide out was usually my apartment. So this chapter covers many visits and conversations. To avoid endless repetition of words and actions, I will state them once. So multiply the actions and statements below by at least 90, and this will approximate how many times I suffered what follows.

Between ten and eleven at night there was a loud knock on my apartment door.

"Oh God, can I come in," pleaded Uranus.

"Sure," I said. "What's up?"

"I just need to escape and hide out from mom for a while," she answered.

Uranus looked a little out of place in her skimpy teenage Tinkerbell jammies, and I wondered if this was going to become a pajama party. Would I need punch and ice-cream? Nope, she brought her own thank you very much, Cherry Garcia and a huge container of Cracker Jacks.

"No sodas please, I only drink milk and water. Got milk?"

So began multiple-hour, non-stop, psycho-babble confession sessions about her slob of a mother and what a huge mistake she had made letting her move in with her again. I felt like a priest in training, without a confession box to sleep in.

Again and again, on each visit, she repeated her life history.

Yet, once in a while she surprised me, by throwing in new and juicy tidbits about her horrid upbringing. Since I am not an ordained Priest, I can tell you about it. She let it out that she had been tossed around like a volleyball, and that her real mother was certifiably insane. Her life had been a nightmare filled with experiences you wouldn't wish on a rabid dog.

"Nana Anna was way better way back then," she said. "She took me in as a Foster child. Now Nana Anna doesn't take care of herself. She has a bad heart and diabetes; she eats all the wrong things, and doesn't take care of her body anymore."

"I have a beautiful body that men crave," Uranus said. "Wouldn't you think she could use me as an example? I'm pretty and men fall in love with me all the time. All men want to have sex with me. Nana Anna used to look as good as me." Then she went on to say that she, miss example, had been an exotic dancer, and later a prostitute. "I've slept with more men than I can count," she noted. Was this bragging? Weird! Why is she telling me this? Uranus went on and on: "When I was serious with this one guy, I found out he cheated on me. So I decided to get even and screwed his brains out. We had hot sex all night and both of us had orgasm after orgasm. I moaned, and panted, and drove him crazy with desire. I'm the piece of the century, and I wanted him to know it. By morning the sheets were completely soaked and stained. I had him begging me to stop. Then I dressed and, as I left, I told him this is what he just lost by cheating on me!" Is that revenge or what? Boy she really got even – NOT! YIKES!

Ok, I was getting a bit sick to my stomach by then, and began wondering just who the hell this narcissistic woman was. She was obviously in love with no one but herself. Her mouth had to have a nuclear power source. She continued to babble non-stop. I just shook my head, yawned, shook my head again, clenched my teeth, bit my tongue, and said to myself OH MY! My kingdom for a confession box or sleep. Yes, sleep is what I need – lots of it.

Uranus jabbered on about her first and only husband, and then about the real father of her children; not the same guy by the way. While still married, she got pregnant with baby Grope by another man. According to her, the father is a Puerto Rican that is not circumcised. YIKES! She told me that she wanted babies more as possessions than children. In the same conversation, Uranus said that she should have given them up, but just couldn't let someone else raise them. "Grope wasn't circumcised, both because it is cleaner that way, and an uncircumcised man gets more pleasure out of sex," she announced. She followed that by saying that Grope never holds his penis when going to the bathroom. "He does the target shooting hip thing, and sprays urine all over the bathroom." I think I groaned at that point. Think Grand Central Station and the subway entrance in New York City! What a visual! YUK!

After Grope was born, Uranus had a second baby, a girl named Tommie, with the same Latino guy. She said, "He never cared for the kids so I wouldn't marry him. He does pay me a little money for child support, but that is taken out by the state as garnished wages, so that doesn't count as support, sharing or caring." She continued, "Besides, he's now gay and living with his lover boyfriend, not that I have anything against gays." Then she said, "The kids can call their father any time they want, and Tommie has his number in her cell phone." Well, you can add another set of lies to the list. We checked Tommie's phone and there is no such number listed.

There were some nights Uranus would disappear and stay out all night. I was thankful. I got some sleep. She told me that sex was her stress reliever and, when really stressed with her mother, Navy boy was her current sex buddy. I am repeating myself here, but this is the moment when she actually told me about Navy boy and the fact that he's the guy she was having carnal knowledge with when the police and Social Services hit her apartment, taking her kids. Shopping for groceries was a just cover story. OH MY! The lie list began growing like Pinocchio's nose, only longer.

Thinking back on the whole beginning of this story, I ask myself over and over, why I didn't chuck her out of my life right then. I am sure it was because of the children. The kids were and are great, despite their problems and special needs. Besides, at this point in time, other events began to take shape that would reel me and Katie further into the quagmire.

CHAPTER 6
TAGS, TAGS, WHERE ARE THE TAGS?

I t was eight in the morning. I was sound asleep. Someone was pounding on my door. I groggily slipped on jeans and stumbled to the door. Peeking through the security hole, I saw a pale oblong face with a distorted beak, squinty blue eyes, and flaming red hair. It had to be Uranus.

"Hurry up. Open the door. Some bastard took the tags off my car," she squeaked. I opened the door, and she came stomping in teary eyed, and mad as a hornet. "The damn police left me a note telling me my out of date tags have been taken." She continued her tantrum by saying, "The seizure of my tags is illegal because my car is parked here on private property." WRONG! Tom, the apartment Maintenance Manager, had spotted the car parked in the lot with expired tags and asked the police to either remove the tags or tow the car. Ooops! She also told me that her vehicle insurance had lapsed.

So, awake and grumpy without my morning coffee, I drove her to the Motor Vehicle Administration office located downtown, and she discovered that she owed over $5,000 in fines for out of date tags and driving without insurance, probably for forever.

She was in tears as I drove her back home. Yes, she had screwed up big time, but didn't have the money to pay for the fines. Nana Anna had already maxed her credit cards to get the apartment, pay for the phone and the utilities.

Uranus continued to whine, "Nana Anna only has a part time job and limited funds. I'm losing my job and security clearance because of that whacko bitch at my old apartment building. I can't ask mom for another penny, because she's too damn controlling, and she'll become even more impossible to live with if I ask her."

Uranus took a deep breath, her face flushing, and repeated once again, "Shit. This situation is all due to my eviction, the fracking child neglect lawsuit, and the bitch that turned me in. Bastards, all of them are bastards!"

"OK, all is not lost," I said, trying to calm her down. "Work a deal to get the car back. Try for a fine reduction, and arrange for scheduled payments through your lawyer, Guido." I also suggested renting a garage here at the complex, and placing the car in it to avoid towing, impounding, and potential loss of the car. This was my good fatherly advice to a reckless woman in trouble. "You can also use my Explorer too, when needed," I offered.

Now cut me a break here. Yes, I was stupid for saying that, but I was trying to be kind. The lady may not be a lady, and she may be crazy, but she and her kids deserved a break.

Thinking back, this woman must be a witch. She can hypnotize anyone and convince them the moon is mars. I admit it; I was down right stupid to offer my car. To prove the point, I found out later that she was actually hauling her dog, Dumpy, in it, even though I had specifically asked her not to. I am allergic to dogs. Phew! Stinky wet dog fur - YUK! I really began to feel used at this point. Plus, I needed my Explorer and did not want to be her chauffer any longer. There had to be a way.

A light bulb clicked on in my brain. Remember my pick up truck, you know, my other truck? I had loaned it to a friend Bob at the local motorcycle store because he had no transportation to and from work. He lived 40 miles away. Bob's truck had recently been totaled in an accident, and he was quite poor, with a sick wife. He had asked to borrow it for a couple of weeks only, and I willingly agreed. He had kept it for over two months. I figured it was time to get it back. Besides, Bob had told me that he was moving back to Alabama soon, and I did not want him driving it there. So, I told Uranus she could use it until I gave it to my grandson or sold it. After Bob returned the vehicle, I found out that, while he had used it, he had really trashed the inside of the truck. He smoked like a chimney, disobeying my request not to smoke in it. In fact, I learned that his buddy, Chuck, carpooled with him to work, and both of them smoked heavily. The truck simply reeked, and the carpets were littered with trash, mud, and covered with grease. I bought the cleaning supplies. Uranus cleaned out the truck until the interior looked and smelled new. She did a great job. So, loaning the truck to Uranus was not a big thing for me, except I was paying the Insurance for her to drive it. That's OK; I got my Explorer back, and the pickup truck cleaned for free. I had the Explorer detailed to remove the doggy stink, and any other Grope droppings, and all was rosy, until the truck battery died. You see, Grope had switched on the overhead lights, which went unnoticed by Uranus for days, and the lights weakened the old battery, and it's difficult to kill a Sears Die-Hard.

Sure enough, Uranus called me one weekday afternoon during rush hour from the City, and said, "The damn truck won't start." She was livid. She was at the some Government building in Manhattan, and I did not want to travel 50 miles in a traffic jam to help her. Uranus finally got a jump, (keep your mind out of the gutter – I mean a battery jump start), and drove the truck back to the local NTB store here in Arrowhead. She called me when she got there. I drove my Explorer to meet her and had the truck battery changed, an expense I was not prepared for. But, the battery was over three years old and probably needed changing anyway.

Oh key doe key, everything was peachy fine for another week. Then the starter died. Yep, I laid out another $250.00 for the starter. This hurt me.

Transportation finally solved for a while, Uranus was now independent from me, and both of us were much happier. However, the loss of her job was looming big on the horizon. So begins the next part of this never ending nightmare.

CHAPTER 7
SLEEPLESS NIGHTS

K nock-Knock! "Who's there?"
"It's Uranus. Who else would be banging on your door at 11:30 at night? Were you asleep? We need to talk."

Crap, I slipped into my Levi's, threw on a T-shirt and opened the door. There she was again; barefoot in her teeny bopper Tinkerbell Jammies, Cherry Garcia in one hand, and a huge container of candy coated popcorn and nuts in the other. Oh my! Another 4 hour session was about to begin. Was this going to be repeat number 91? ARRRGGHH! I would have dropped everything then and there and locked the door if I had known then what I know now. The frustration was only just beginning to emerge.

To my amazement, another topic was brought up out of the blue. She announced, "I must find another job and right away. I squeezed my employer for as much pay as I can get. I'll be let go any day."

In truth, she was exaggerating. She was laid off a couple of months later. Even then, she received some severance pay. Uranus was employed by the Federal Government, and she was really good at milking money from them— either that or her boss is a big sucker, getting some, or both.

"It has to be a Government job because that's all I want," she announced with adamant determination in her voice.

I said, "It may be impossible for you to work for the

Government without any clearance – except in some less important areas." I gently suggested, "You can find a commercial job right here. With your office skills, there are many available jobs close to home, and they pay well."

"No fracking way" she replied, "Government or nada!" And in the same breath she asked: "Can I use your computer to search for jobs?"

"Hunh? What about using the computer in the Business Center, right here in the Apartment complex?" I countered. "After all, it's next door."

"Oh, I plan to do that during the day. I mean use yours at night. You have a printer and all. Plus, you stay up late and I need to get away from mom – she's driving me crazy." GROAN!

So, with the patience of Job, yet with many reservations, I caved in again. "I guess that's OK for now," I said.

My past wife use to call me "sucker man." Wow, was she right. Little did I know what "OK for now" really implied. It meant she would be sitting at my PC desk, in my bedroom, virtually every night until 4AM for the next two months, and I would wind up sleeping on the lumpy old couch in my living room until I couldn't stand it anymore!

So, the agonizing process began with her searching databases for all of the Government jobs available in the entire world, printing reams of paper, and filling my bedroom/office with notebook after notebook, in the attempt of locating "just the perfect Government job," that would make her big bucks. Search aside; it also took three full weeks for her to organize a basic résumé. I mean, "BASIC" résumé. She told me, "I'm an expert at developing Government résumé's." Why so much material? Did she include every conversation she had with everyone since she first began work? Did she include every task she was asked to do, every letter she ever typed, every note she had taken in meetings, every trip to the restroom? Let's get real.

She was a fracking secretary (I am not knocking secretaries here, as they are valuable assets). Three weeks of endless nights and over forty pages for a résumé? Then Uranus began to tailoring résumé's for each of the jobs she had listed. This became exasperating to the max!

I was wondering why she had not sent any résumé's out yet, and I approached her on the topic. "Why is this taking so long?" I asked. She constantly made lame excuses. She was very good at that. Politics – that's her calling. Egad.

One night around 2 AM, I quietly entered my bedroom/office, and observed that she was on chat with a bunch of her old military boyfriends, from the west coast or wherever. The light bulb went on again. This enlightenment blew my mind. I gritted my teeth and gently but firmly informed her that she would never find a job at this rate, and she must drop the chat crap and get to the search. She said she would.

Then I began asking her to leave around 11 PM because I was tired of my lumpy couch. She always put me off until at least 2 AM. I knew Uranus was sneaking in Chat sessions and Alt_Tab hiding them when I came into the room to check. I caught her at this a number of times, spotting the chat line on the taskbar. The whole "sneaking" situation was getting old fast. To make a not-so-subtle hint, I told her that I was going to bed because the couch was not comfortable and my back was hurting. Did this strike home? WHAT PART OF LEAVE AT 11 DON'T YOU UNDERSTAND?

I snore. Yes! Yank off the Breath Easy strips. This will do the trick – NOT. She must have purchased earplugs. She still stayed on the computer until 4 AM, and bailed out long after I had fallen asleep, leaving her empty Cherry Garcia tubs and Cracker Jack containers on or under my desk. This became ritual; me sleeping in my clothes, snoring like a buzz saw, and Uranus chatting her skinny ass off with her list of internet military boyfriends, making absolutely no progress on her job search.

Many late nights later, I discovered that Uranus was not looking for local Government jobs at all. She had stumbled upon an epiphany. "I can make big bucks by going overseas – like to Iraq. I can work for Halliburton or some company like that – as a contractor. There are job openings. I can work one year and come back debt free and regain my clearance and buy a new sports car and maybe a house and live in a manner to which I deserve."

Yeah right!

She went on to say, "During my breaks I can take the kids on exotic vacations like to Viet Nam, Mainland China, or Cambodia. I always wanted to go there and it will be culturally good for the kids."

Yeah, that and the bird flu will be just great, I thought.

Her psycho-babble continued, "I can send the kids to summer camps and to their original home in Kansas for visits." I guess she thought she could make $1000 an hour and work 96 hour weeks to pay for all of this. She was becoming delusional. Did I say "becoming?"

"What about the kids?" I asked.

"Nana Anna will watch them," she replied.

"Now wait a minute," I said. "You told me before that Nana Anna is totally incompetent, a slob, sick, sleeps all the time and is totally incapable of watching the children. You must find someone else, Uranus." I was becoming very upset. This was totally irrational of her – YOU THINK?

Uranus would hear absolutely none of this. She had made up her puny little mind. Overseas was the perfect out for her, the perfect escape. It was at this point I FINALLY realized she was nutty as a fruitcake - an epiphany for me? Nah! A brain fart is more like it. I had been a fool and so badly used. We all had.

Uranus rambled on, "I will create a work list for the kids and a watch list for you guys to help Nana Anna. You and Katie and Tack and Booby will be my support group and yada, yada, yada can take the kids to appointments, movies, parks, and on special trips" In other words – we can become the doting parents while she was off on holiday. Did we know that she had a boyfriend waiting for her in Iraq? No we did not. But she did: a big stiff legged fireman all ready to rock and roll.

"I will get the car license paid and fix up the vehicle so Nana Anna can drive."

YEAH RIGHT!

"I will create Powers of Attorney so all of you in the support group, can handle the kid's appointments, and Nana Anna will be in charge - she likes being in charge."

This was getting thick, deep, and reeking of escape plan number 69. Her id and her horns were raging.

What woman in her right mind would volunteer to leave her kids for a year, much worse with another woman that has serious heart and diabetes problems; a woman she had kicked out of her home once before because she is a total slob, and someone she constantly complained about for the past several months since she moved her back in? Now, I'll be honest here. I understood her basic reasoning for taking a high paying job, and actually agreed with her **if** she carefully planned her expenditures, paid off all of her debt, and carefully watched her money, and most importantly found the right person to watch the children. If she stuck with this plan, working in Iraq might be in the kids' best interest. Other than that, the plan appeared to be totally self-serving. We all realize today that she had probably been planning this leap from responsibility for some time – long before or just after her arrest. Ooops, I am getting ahead of myself again.

CHAPTER 8
DECEIT AND BARE FACTS

I uncovered Mr. Pervert by pure accident. Uranus asked me to help deceive an old Army boyfriend, the best sex of her life, according to her. He was the perfect man for her and her kids. She wanted him back. Uranus had found him on the internet in a Chat arena while working hard on her job search (oxy moron somewhere in here). She had been communicating with him for a while now at night, and was using a new User ID to keep him from finding out just who she was. Apparently, Uranus had met this guy some time ago and on the first date had really hot sex with him. Immediately afterward, the guy dumped her for some unknown reason (smart fellow). He was also married now, but waiting for his wife to arrive in the US from Cambodia or Thailand or some exotic country like that. His being married didn't matter to Uranus. She could get him back. He was hers for the taking. She tried to convince him to annul the marriage and come to Arrowhead to live with her and the kids. She was having great internet sex with him, and wanted to take a real trip to the sack with him to convince the poor bastard that there was no other woman in the world that could satisfy him like her. He, in turn, wanted pictures of her, and that is where I came in. GROAN! At the time I was unaware of any of the details, other than he was not to find out who she was. I was reluctant, but I caved in and took a number of digital pictures of her dressed in different outfits. I did this as quickly as I could, not really caring how the photos turned out. She, in turn, filtered through the photos on my computer for hours, and finally picked out what she thought to be the most sexy, but illusive picture she could find. Through software enhancement, her hair and eye color were changed to brown, and her face was half hidden and blurred. Her boney, flat chested figure was revealed in a flimsy pixie-like dress, not nasty, but sexy, and yes, she did wear underwear.

So she emailed the picture, a very tiny one about one inch square. He was not happy at all.

Mr. Pervert is married, yet he replied to the email, wanting body shots and close up nude shots of her private parts, and whatever else she was willing to give up. NO WAY JOSE! Not on my watch. Not with my camera or PC.

Uranus told me that on a previous occasion and on another PC she had taken a number of X-Rated private-part nude and sex shots using her fingers and a vibrator. She sent the photos over the internet. She kept the shots on a CD somewhere, and probably published them on the internet. I wanted no part of that crap. That would never have happened anyway. She said that her only concern about nasty nude shots was that I might see something I shouldn't see, as if I would ever look at that kind of picture of her – GROSS! YUK! Well, I might peek at them; after all, I am a male. Nah! No way! My wife would come back from the grave and haunt me.

To make this long story short, the sordid internet affair continued for a couple of weeks, and I constantly advised her to let the cat out of the bag. "He will eventually find out," I said. "Lies find a way of coming to the surface." I was totally sick of the fiasco, and sick of her stubborn determination. Uranus needed to concentrate on finding a job and the right person to watch the children, but she was literally possessed with this perverted jerk. Late one night, she finally caved in to my demands and did tell him who she was. Mr. Pervert dumped her the next day. What does that tell you? I was relieved. She was pissed. One of the most embarrassing ordeals of my life was finally over.

Just how the hell I had gotten mixed up in this nasty mess in the first place nagged me to no end. I felt used and abused, albeit I volunteered. Yep! Sucker man to the rescue! AGAIN! It was my stupid fault. From this point on I didn't respect her at all, but I still cared for the kids. I had to maintain that perspective.

So the sleepless nights continued, Uranus got back to work on her search, and finally KBR sent her a letter in the mail. She ran down stairs to show it to me. They offered her a job in Iraq. Then the real nightmare officially began to unfold.

CHAPTER 9
HERE COMES THE JUDGE

D ressed to the nines, Uranus and her lawyer appeared in court for the criminal proceedings, the first of two child neglect hearings to be held resulting from her prior arrest. The hearing, however, turned out to be a joke. Child Protective Services was totally unprepared and the contract lawyer that represented them, having been assigned the case the day before, was literally eaten alive by Uranus's lawyer, Guido. The Judge listened to all that was said, reprimanded the police and CPS, pounded his gavel and formally dismissed the criminal hearing. He said "I will review the case, and report back to everyone in a week or so."

A few weeks later, the Judge released his findings. There was no surprise. The police and Social Workers had entered the apartment without a warrant. All were reprimanded in writing by the Judge. Entry and seizure of the children by Social Services was deemed to be totally illegal by the Judge. The Judge dismissed the case, and returned full custody of the children to the mom.

In a later appeals hearing, one that Uranus did not attend, the Judge also expunged the entire criminal case from Uranus' record. However, the neglect hearing was still an open issue and yet to be held.

Guido was beside himself, polishing his own apple, stating what a clever job he had done. He actually dropped by my apartment to show me how much testimony he had expunged from the hearing record. The dropped material would not be allowed in the follow-up Social Services neglect hearing. He showed me a fist full of paper with blacked out lines throughout. He had removed most of the testimony, and all of the evidentiary proof.

Guido said, "The CPS neglect hearing will be a breeze."

It was at this meeting in my apartment when Guido admitted to me that he knew Uranus was mentally ill and seriously in need of psychiatric help. I asked him why he was representing her, and he replied, "I signed up for the criminal case, and now I must to follow through, even though this type of case is out of my element. After all, I am a criminal lawyer and that is why I took on the case in the first place. I won that side of the case. I need to hang in there with her. We'll win the next one too"

I wondered why he was sticking with her. Was he that hard up for money? Was it something else? It must be all the free Five Guys Burgers she was buying him.

So much for the kids, the criminal hearing was over. STRIKE ONE for the good guys! Back to normal for now, or I should say back to abnormal. What would be the outcome of the neglect hearing? We would need to wait and see.

CHAPTER 10
I WAS BLIND, NOW I CAN SEE

Tommie's school grades were dismal at best, and had been most of her life. Through total coincidence, we learned that she could neither read nor do math. Why the schools had not caught this was simply amazing to us. Actually, Uranus knew of this problem, but always made it clear to the kids that school homework, attendance, and behavior was their responsibility, not hers. Uranus could give a damn about school. Tommie was literally blind and could not read. She needed glasses in the worst way.

Tommie has a most wonderful personality, and appears normal in all ways, until we uncovered the facts about her so called learning disabilities. It was not difficult for us to discover. She couldn't read a simple first grade book. Well, strike another winner for Uranus. She knew that Tommie had vision problems and needed glasses. She knew that Tommie's eyesight was dismal at best, but correctable. Instead of glasses for her daughter, Uranus decided that "they" needed a new pet, a Chinchilla – complete with expensive cage and what all. Besides, Uranus didn't have the time to bother with trips to an eye doctor. Tommie could just tough it out for now.

You now can see that Uranus did not like spending Child Support money on anything except for her wants and needs. But, under pressure, Uranus finally caved in, having been convinced by us that the glasses would mostly be paid by

Tommie's father, Curly. He had vision insurance. She made the appointments and payment arrangements by phone just before departing for Iraq, leaving the day trips to her support group.

After a few weeks Tommie picked up her new glasses. Tommie was amazed that she could actually see things like never before. She could even read a few road signs on the way home, at least some of the words. It was amazing to her, like a new world. The plastic, black rimmed glasses even looked cute on her. Of course we, the support group, were the ones that took her to get all this done. Thanks for nothing Uranus. Please go Iraq, step on an IED somewhere. Better yet, stuff a grenade up your derrière and pull the pin.

Tommie could now see, but still not read or do math. She needed special help and soon.

CHAPTER 11
BAIL OUT

The parachute was packed and it was nearing time to bail. There was no convincing Uranus that she was making terrible choices, and that it was a really bad time to leave her children. I knew she had other options; so did she. In fact, she had told me about another job offer locally. But then she said, "The job requires me to eventually get a security clearance. There's no way for me to get another clearance yet, because of my bad credit." Uranus could easily have elected to leave at a later time, but she would not hear of it. She used the lame excuse, "The sooner I go, the sooner I'll be back." I know for fact that she could have delayed her departure, leaving sufficient time to find a suitable child care provider. But she repeated over and over, "Nana Anna can do it; the kids will just have to tough it out."

This was her final response. What I did not know at the time was the first hearing Judge had told Uranus and Guido that the children required full time supervision. Being autistic with Asperger's Syndrome, Grope was to never be left alone without adult supervision. Nana Anna worked. Uranus had lied to the court, telling them that Nana Anna did not work. Of course there were lots of other things I didn't know at the time, and later, as the fog cleared so to speak, Uranus's open disregard of the law became more and more evident.

In late March, Uranus flew to Houston for three weeks of

testing and training. As it turned out, the training time was cut short because she was "needed in Iraq." In fact, she had escaped the entire Psychological testing phase, and bragged about it later by email, because she knew she would have failed. Did she know she was nuts? I would say consciously no. However, the truth festered in the subterranean portion of her pea sized brain.

The initial week or two on the home front was very hard on Nana Anna, in part because she worked. The kids, although still in school, were on the loose and unsupervised while at home, and they would not listen or cooperate with her in the least. The situation became much worse as time passed. Due to lack of doggie walking, Dumpy continued her pooping and urinating all over the apartment. Since the mess was not cleaned up, poop and urine became embedded into the carpet. Grope did not make an attempt to walk around it, even when barefoot. To make matters worse, after wearing their clothes for days on end, the kids dumped their filthy clothes on the floor, letting the clothes soak up some of the poop and urine. The house reeked. Food and other unmentionable stuff was smeared everywhere, and Grope was increasing deposits of his own feces on the walls of his bedroom, peeing all over the bathroom (great hip shots – "yeah, got that fly on the wall)," and taking mechanical and electrical things apart, like the DVD and TV. How the hell he did this while hanging onto a large bionnacle with his left hand I will never know. Yep, curious Grope, rather destructive Grope, was unattended and free to go and do whatever he wanted, even walking a few miles from home to a stream and big pond to catch bugs and pollywogs. He ate the bugs of course, "yummy snacks," and carried the pollywogs home to die and rot somewhere in his room.

Grope had also asked mommy to send him a pet camel spider from Iraq. Uranus said that she would do what she could do. In fact, she did him send one, but it was dead and encased in solid plastic, aw shucks! Personally, I was hoping he would ask for a live cobra, but that was a mean thought. Grope is just Grope, a weird, not-so-little boy with the behavior pattern of a confused and unsupervised OCD, Autistic six year old.

I repeat, I still was unaware that the court had ordered that Grope was never to be left alone. I should have guessed. But it had been covered up by Uranus, and the second court hearing had not even taken place yet. **Court Hearing?** The light clicked on. Did Uranus escape the country early to avoid the second court hearing? She was cunning to the core. The sneak had **Bailed Out!**

CHAPTER 12
THE TOOTH FAIRY

Tommie is a beautiful eleven year old tom boy, complete with a missing front tooth, scraped up arms and knees from tree climbing, skateboarding, and other sporting fun. One of her top front teeth had been knocked out while playing on the rings at school. It took a lot of convincing to make Uranus make an appointment with an Orthodontist. She was pissed off because she would rather have used the child support money on a new dress she had seen on the internet. Plus, she also wanted to buy some $40 cookie treats and tootsie warmers for Dumpy. After all, it was still winter.

As for the tooth, Uranus had scheduled an appointment with a Dentist to take place after she had bailed to Iraq. This plan worked out best for her, because she had been able to arrange for Curly to pay the bill, thereby saving the expense on her Child Support Card, while avoiding the inconvenience of having to take Tommie to the dentist herself. Yep! The internet dress was hers, and she ordered it, and she bought the cookies and tootsie warmers for Dumpy.

Of course, since Curly was paying the bill, an ordinary bridge would not do. Tommie must have an implant. What Uranus did not realize at the time was that an implant could not be placed in her mouth until Tommie turned at least sixteen. She needed something temporary until then.

What Tommie did receive was a horrid Rube-Goldberg metal

bridge, complete with an ugly dark grey tooth. The deed was done by a totally incompetent dentist, not a specialist. With the distorted bridge jammed into her mouth, Tommie spoke like she had her tongue tied to the roof of her mouth.

"Ith awfill an it hurth," she complained bitterly.

Uranus was informed of this problem by email, from both Katie and me, and Uranus simply replied in her very best mommy dearest writing, "Tell her to stop her damn complaining and just let her tough it out."

For the longest time, Tommie appeared toothless more often than not, and it was no surprise to any of us, because the device irritated her no end. I remembered a temporary front tooth bridge I had been given when young, and it had driven me crazy. I conveniently lost it. Well, so did Tommie. "I was in the woods with Grope catching frogs and it must have fell outa my pocket when I jumped over a big puddle," she innocently said, looking at us with her pretty brown eyes, wide and semi-convincing. Tommie was becoming as good a fibber as her freaky mother. Yep! We all knew that Tommie had a great teacher. Come to think of it, I recall mine fell out of my pocket while crossing the street and the bridge got run over by a truck, or did I accidentally flush it down the toilet? Yes, I was sympathetic. Tommie deserved to lose that horrible tooth.

A second bridge was ordered, through a real Orthodontist this time, and all of us placed bets on how long it would last. However, Uranus told Tommie that if she lost this one, she would go toothless until she was sixteen. She meant it too, even though her perfectly straight teeth would become badly deformed.

Fortunately, the new tooth fit perfectly and looked wonderful. Once again, Tommie had a beautiful smile and no longer hurt or needed to feel embarrassed. Since the bridge was much smaller and fit nicely in her mouth, Tommie took much better care of it. The last I heard, she still has it.

CHAPTER 13
COZY QUARTERS

E mail 1 of 1,000:
"Hello everyone, I'm in Iraq at Camp Fallujah. I am in my hooch and met my roommate. She was nice at first but after I talked to her for a while, she became a bitch." I don't understand!

How about: Entire life story in 40 minutes, including leaving the kids with incompetent Nana Anna et al – go figure.

The emails get better. "I am the prettiest girl here, so the men are all treating me like a queen. I love my boss, but I think he's gay. I am also the most experienced woman here (that's a given). My job is way cool, but it is 120 degrees here and dusty. Can you send my stuff? I sent you a five page list. Just go upstairs to my apartment, and you can find most everything – the rest you can pick up at the following stores yada, yada, and yada."

Yeah! And I can rent a cargo plane to send your crap to you, I thought.

She continued, "I need to buy a bunch of expensive stuff to make the hooch really me, but I will buy that on the internet."

I decided that the kids could find "the stuff." I did not want to go upstairs, and I was not really welcome there, because I think Nana Anna was ashamed of the ever growing mess. Besides, I didn't have a big enough water heater to wash off whatever might get on me if I did go up there. As it turned out, it took a couple of months before I received anything to mail

Uranus from the kids – phew! Nana Anna wasn't going to help. It was up to the kids. Yep - great cooperation by the kids! I did send what they brought me, a huge box of CDs and some tubes of stuff I didn't recognize.

Oh, by the way. Do you remember the notarized Power of Attorney papers for the "Support Group" she typed on my computer at 4 AM? You guessed it.

Email 3 of 1,000:

"Sorry I forgot to have them notarized, you can have Tack's wife do it because she is a lawyer and a notary and she said she would."

HELLO! What part of illegal don't you understand! "I will need to send the papers to you," I replied in a response email.

"Have them notarized by JAG. They have a rep there."

Email 6 of 1,000:

"Remember to not let mom know I gave Tommie the credit card so she can go get $60 haircuts and other stuff she really needs. Nana Anna is too cheap to let her have quality stuff. Katie or you can sneak her out, and you can sign my name on the debit slip." NOT ON YOUR LIFE, KIDDO!

Then the email went on to bash Nana Anna for about 10,000 more words. After reading her psycho babble for what seemed like hours, I prayed Uranus had only one working finger, so she would type slower; She has very quick fingers (oh yeah), quick hands (oh yeah), quick mouth (oh yeah), and no morals – that's Uranus.

Email 12 of 1,000:

"Hey, I have a new roommate. She's a bitch too. I just do not understand. At first she was really nice, now she hates me. Well, I can hardly wait for a single. Then I can fix it up the way I want."

I wanted so badly to send her needle and thread and tell her to sew them up (at least two of her orifices – her choice).

CHAPTER 14
KEYS, KEYS, WHO GETS THE KEYS

Chauffeuring was getting very old for all of us. I queried Uranus about her car that was rotting in her garage. You know, the one she promised to license and repair for Nana Anna to use. "She needs the car," I wrote. "The support group has been forced to take her everywhere, and we are tired of it." Uranus wrote back saying, "I would prefer that "mom" not use the car." However, she requested that I go to MVA for her and help work out the issues so she could make scheduled payments to eventually pay off the debt. She told me that she had sent MVA $1,200, a partial payment, so I should be able to get the tags. For Nana Anna's sake as well as our freedom, I did go to MVA.

Boy was the MVA rude, nasty and arrogant to the max. The guy I dealt with must have caught PMS from the rest of the female staff, or been embarrassed about his totally hairless head.

"We have no record of payment," he stated in a lippy, arrogant tone of voice. "If she sent any money, she must have sent the payment to the wrong place. It MUST be sent to this office."

Baldy continued: "Furthermore, Uranus must come in herself and sign a contract with us before we will do anything for her."

"HELLO! She is in Iraq. You know – WAR ZONE! Can we

just send her the paperwork? JAG will notarize it"

"Absolutely NOT, she must sign in person. End of conversation." With that, he stiffly walked away from me and said in a loud, nasty voice, "NEXT."

Damn County Government employees – what morons. Baldy must have failed geography class. I bet he thought Iraq was just south of town, maybe in Pennsylvania. Yeah, she is going to fly back to the US to sign a contract on a car she doesn't want Nana Anna to drive. Deadbeat!

I emailed Uranus and told her in no uncertain terms to get her lawyer, Guido, involved. I was done with this crap. She did. To my amazement, after numerous attempts over a couple of weeks, Guido hit a stone wall too. Mr. PMS held his ground. He was just as rude to Guido, maybe more so. So Nana Anna would not get the car. Uranus got her wish. She was still in control. We were the chauffeurs – damn! I wondered if she had planned this before she left (maybe I was getting paranoid at this point). Nana Anna knew I was on this task and kept asking "WHEN?" I felt so bad for her and for us. Finally, I had to break the news that the car was not forthcoming, and she would need to continue taking the bus and the subway to and from work, and ask us to help her out when necessary. We really would help where we could. In fact, I had been taking her to the Subway in the morning during rush hour for several weeks.

You might be thinking, what about loaning Nana Anna your pickup truck? First of all, it is a stick shift and Nana Anna can't drive a stick. Secondly, I had already given it to my Grandson.

CHAPTER 15
HERE COMES THE JUDGE

"Where is Uranus," asked the Judge?

"Working, your honor," replied Guido. "She is unable to leave work to get here." Good move, Guido. It would have been hard for her to get to the courtroom from Iraq, and the Judge would have dropped the hammer if he found out she was out of the country. Guido had told all of us that under no circumstances should we tell anyone that Uranus was in Iraq. It would have been fun to announce, but, since the courtroom was closed to the public, we didn't have a chance to speak up.

Guido, having communicated her absence to the court, opened the floor for the prosecution to move for an immediate entry of GUILTY! Unfortunately, the Judge refused the Guilty verdict, and ordered the hearing to proceed. But it turned out not to matter anyway. It was just another waste of everyone's time.

I did not get the word from CPS, but I did receive the neglect hearing court judgment papers from Nana Anna a few weeks later. **GUILTY – all counts!** The judgment papers stated that Uranus shall remain on the "child neglect" list for years to come. Again, the court reiterated that the children must receive full time supervision, which, of course, they were not receiving. Unfortunately, CPS failed to report this fact to the court. Actually, this order carried over from the earlier criminal hearing. We were sure that CPS had not even checked into Nana Anna's job status.

Yep, Uranus lost the CPS neglect case. Guido told me on a later visit to my apartment that he had expected Uranus would be found guilty. Come to think of it, hadn't he said this hearing would be a no-brainer? With a smile on my face, I gave Guido his copies of the hearing notes and judgments, scanned and emailed another set to Uranus, and returned the originals back to Nana Anna. To this day, Uranus claims the entire record had been expunged by the Court – how 'bout that for total denial, selective memory. Of course, I kept scanned copies. Uranus had asked me to, and I was happy to oblige.

So here we are folks. summer has arrived, well almost. The kids remain unsupervised while Nana Anna works. Memorial Day has passed, and the Apartment Complex pool is open. Nothing else is new. The situation between Nana Anna and Uranus worsens day by day. Hate mail from Uranus enters my email box daily. She writes endless ranting and ravings about how Nana Anna is screwing up the kids both mentally and physically. She complains that Nana Anna is not answering her emails. I checked with her. Nana Anna had not received a single email yet from Uranus. We slither into the deeper stages of psychotic madness emanating from Iraq, and I am not referring to the war.

CHAPTER 16
RANTING AND RAVINGS

I was becoming saturated and totally flustered with gigabytes of email from Uranus complaining about Nana Anna, and that she was the root of all her problems. Nana Anna was trashing the house, and the kids wouldn't help because Nana Anna wasn't doing her fair share. And, to make matters worse, the kids were eating out all the time, ingesting all the wrong foods. Total nonsense! Uranus had no idea that we were taking Nana Anna to the Supermarket to buy wholesome food. Uranus had asked questions of the children and they told her "exactly" what she wanted to hear. They were playing her like a Stradivarius.

On one of her daily phone calls from Iraq, Uranus asked Tommie to use her camera phone and take pictures of the apartment, then send them to her over the internet. The apartment looked like a sewer. Tommie complied, and Uranus immediately proceeded to send the photos to her entire email address book, even to Nana Anna's boss at work. Uranus' entire escape plan was self-destructing at light speed, and she was doing it to herself by stating the obvious; Uranus had screwed up and deserted her kids.

Dumpy wasn't being taken of care at all, or walked like Uranus demanded. The urine and poop damage was getting worse and worse throughout the apartment. Grope was getting really good at squishing the poop into the carpet, then throwing clothes on top to cover the stink. It didn't matter if the clothes were clean or dirty.

To help reduce the problem, Nana Anna cleaned up and bought pee pads. She strategically placed them around the apartment. This solution started to work. But Uranus was furious with this solution, and told Nana Anna to get rid of the pee pads immediately and simply clean up the fracking mess and walk the dog. Finally, Nana Anna stood up for herself and screamed into the phone. "Then tell your damn kids to cooperate and walk the damn dog," This statement fell upon deaf ears.

Uranus' daily torment of Nana Anna was building like a hurricane in the tropics. The kids were not helping in the least; the doggie was suffering, and Uranus was totally blinded - believing only what she wanted to see and hear. Her mind was rotting with malignant rage, and she refused to take the appropriate action, obvious to any sane and caring person. She should quit her damn job and come home. Home is where she belonged. Screw Iraq. Her selfish plan was NOT working and she damn well knew it.

Email 35 of 1,000:

"Would you please convince Nana Anna to apply for Disability Insurance and Social Security Disability so she can go back home? I am sure she could qualify. I want her out of my life, and I will find someone else to watch the kids."

I sent Uranus a detailed email on what it would take to qualify Nana Anna for both Disability Insurance and Social Security Disability. I know from personal experience what it takes because I became permanently disabled two years back, and went through the maze of physicals, evaluations, and paperwork to qualify. My vascular condition is far more severe than Nana Anna's ever was, and my situation is inoperable. According to what Nana Anna told me, her health condition is not only controllable, but correctable. Regardless, I carefully detailed all of the options to Nana Anna, who was becoming a friend of sorts after hauling her around in my car for so long, as well as daily chats at the mailbox. In truth, she would not qualify easily. There was a very slim chance, and I did not know the Government regulations or whether she could qualify for Disability Insurance as a part time employee of the Government. So I suggested to her that she make an appointment with an Independent Vocational Specialist (MD) for a complete evaluation. As with all of the other suggestions the support group made to her, she ignored the advice and the appointment never happened. I felt the outcome was predictable anyway. She didn't have a chance.

Uranus' plan du jour was to secretly find a suitable replacement for Nana Anna. Suitable, being the operative word, meant to Uranus "anyone" she could find. She said, "Nana Anna can live at home for the time being, only if she allows me continued use of her checkbook, credit card, and phone. In addition, Nana Anna must agree to be totally under my control, since I am supporting her and paying all of the bills."

Boy this really made sense – NOT! WWIII would happen first. Uranus already owed Nana Anna a fortune. Besides, I saw receipts where Nana Anna was currently paying past due bills out of her own pocket. Both Nana Anna and Uranus are stubborn beyond belief, but Nana Anna is most likely sane, and Uranus is mentally ill, living in an imaginary world of her own.

Uranus' first replacement choice was a girlfriend that she knew from her former place of employment. That idea flopped miserably when Uranus found out that her "friend" was shacking up with a new boyfriend and had absolutely no interest in screwing up her new relationship with someone else's messed up kids.

Her second choice was the brother of Curly, the father of the children. Actually Moe, Curly's brother, by outward appearances seemed to be a decent guy, but he had been out of work for two years because of ID theft by a convicted criminal. Moe had just been hired by the FAA somewhere in the Midwest. Nevertheless, Uranus was determined she could convince Moe to do it – quit his new job, move across country, and slip right in. Maybe he could work for the FAA in Atlantic City and commute daily, i.e. never home. I thought Uranus had a better chance hiring an old prostitute girlfriend from the Trenton slums. Her request of Moe was totally self serving and unfair. What was she doing to her family (if you can call it that)?

Of course, her friend Booby could do it too, as a backup; but the courts could never find out. YEAH: The kids, doggie, Chinchilla, and whatever could fit into Booby's tiny, two bedroom apartment, complete with husband, two kids of her own, and cats; Mmmmmmm, yummy lunch for doggie and little girls for Grope to sleep with in the same bedroom. What a thought!

Then there was another single, pregnant friend up north of the City, somewhere near White Plains, that could take at least one of them if need be. Nah! That wouldn't work. Who would watch the other one?

Then she started posting notes on the internet claiming "free living expenses in return for watching two well behaved children." Oh my! No takers there. Well, she did get one query. It was a lady from the same church. She backed out after talking to Uranus for about five minutes.

I guess by now you see the picture – the id was raging and she didn't care where the kids wound up, together or apart. Uranus was intent on remaining in Iraq where she had no responsibilities, made big bucks, could spend money freely, and get laid all she wanted by her "fireman" boyfriend or whomever else was handy at the time.

CHAPTER 17
FETISH AND CRAVINGS

At this juncture the key problem with "proper" food (as defined by Uranus) was that Grope, a growing carnivorous teenager, was left home alone most of the day and he would eat everything in sight, then leave leftovers scattered all over the walls, floors, and counters. There was rarely edible food left in the house when Nana Anna arrived home. No wonder they ate out a lot. Nana Anna was too tired to go to the grocery store every day.

Grope was also well established with his poop smearing frenzy, and having the absolute best time tormenting Dumpy. He pulled her around by the tail and ears, and held her down, sucking and licking her private parts: "here doggie, doggie – yummy, yummy!" Slurp, Slurp!

He admitted his behavior openly. In fact, he bragged about it.

When I confronted Uranus with Grope's habitual poop smearing on walls, dog sucking and tormenting fetish, as well as his bug eating, she replied to me by email to stop the Grope bashing.

She wrote, "My boy is a perfectly normal thirteen year-old. All of the Damned Psychiatrists, Psychologists, Sociologists, and the other doctors and so-called professionals that have evaluated him in the past don't know their ass from a groundhog hole." Uranus rambled on, "As far as his poop smearing goes, Grope likes animals and is just emulating them by marking his territory. And he would never hurt Dumpy, either. He loves Dumpy." She finished this email by writing, "I am the only person that knows what was right and best for my son." Yep, only Uranus has the remedy. Folks, she is in total psychotic denial!

She wrote the following in another sick email, "Encourage him to eat bugs and let him spread his shit. He has been doing that stuff forever. Besides, the bugs are good for him and Nana Anna is probably not giving him enough protein to eat. As for the shit, just make him clean up his poop mess afterwards. He will if you stand over him until he is done. Understanding and encouragement is the key."

Yeah, right, and the spray that has been placed on the bushes where he picks the bugs is especially nutritious. The poop smell, and pee on the walls and floors just add aroma to his room and the apartment. The stairway in the NYC Penn Station Subway entrance is cleaner, and probably smells better.

Uranus is totally delusional to think that any one of us would live up there while he was left alone, much worse, stand over him while he cleans up his shit. The boy needs full time supervision, professional help. Supervision had been ordered by the court. Disrespect for her within the support group was growing fast, because Uranus refused to obey the law and follow the courts directions. Her behavior toward the kids and everyone else was pathetic. Of course Tack and Booby, both of whom we never saw, were oblivious to her psychotic behavior. Katie, Nana Anna and I talked about her condition often, and all agreed that she is, indeed, mentally ill and in need of professional help more than the kids.

CHAPTER 18
SPEND, SPEND, SPEND
'TIL YOUR MOMMY TAKES YOUR
CHECKBOOK AWAY

There is a little "Beach Boys" in the Chapter title somewhere. I know that's lame, but that's a line for us older folks I just couldn't pass on. The Beach Boys still ROCK! Or have they retired? I forget.

Remember, Uranus had given us permission to examine her accounts. Nana Anna was also on top of her spending because it was actually her account, and she could ask for records. Uranus could not get an account of her own because of her bad credit history. She was also mathematically impaired or just didn't give a rat's ass about her mother's bank account, into which she was supposedly depositing money for expenses and paying bills.

For some reason, Uranus' State Tax payment bounced three times before it cleared. She did not bother to check for funds available. Uranus was not paying attention to her other spending either. She forgot about all the internet purchases she had recently made to fancy up her hooch, treat her hair and skin, special doggie yummies for Dumpy, expensive treats for the Chinchilla, oversized boy clothes for Tommie, and Camel spiders and other desert books and creatures for Grope. Of course, she had also written a check for a week long "Surf Camp" vacation for Tommie that cost a couple of thousand bucks. Checks were bouncing on a regular basis, Nana Anna's credit was being affected, and the bank threatened to close her account. This behavior by Uranus was NOT taking care of the car issue or paying off her debts – you know – the "plan." There was no plan. Uranus was free and had no responsibilities to worry about. She was on a spending frenzy.

Over time money went out as fast as or faster than it came in. Checks continued to bounce and Nana Anna continued being harassed by the Bank. Meanwhile, the car sat in the garage rotting. What made it embarrassing for Nana Anna and hard on us was the fact that she was still totally dependent on all of us for her to go anywhere. Uranus had her head in the sand, or somewhere dark and stinky, and her hand on the credit card, Ka-Ching.

CHAPTER 19
RING, RING, THREE TIMES A DAY

I must regress here a little bit. Just before Uranus left for Iraq, Katie and family had moved from Uranus' old apartment building into a nice apartment across the street from us. This was good news, being close. As a courtesy, Tommie was being driven to and from school daily by Katie, because both Katie and Uranus wanted to leave their kids in their original school to finish out the semester. That's a good thing. Now, you must understand that Katie, being a long-term Navy wife, has a great reputation for timeliness and always leaves early and arrives on or ahead of schedule. That also is a good thing. Tommie, however, believes that being late is an accomplishment. She learned that trait from her mom. Later is better. There is a certain pride in it. You know the type – the last one on the airplane, "Hold the doors I'm on the ramp!" Well, that's not a good thing. It's downright rude.

Now let's move forward a bit to the time when school was still in session, but nearly over. Katie was still transporting Tommie to and from school. Uranus had only been in Iraq for a very short time. She had just been given her own office phone and could call home whenever she wanted over a special KBR line. The event that happened during this period, just before the summer break, set the stage for future problems, major ones.

We know that oil and water do not mix. Something had to give and it wasn't going to be Katie. Tommie had been warned by Katie a number of times that she had better be on time or she would no longer take her to and from school. The threat became a challenge to Tommie, to see how far she could push Katie. For the next few days, Katie watched Tommie standing on the curb across the street from her parking lot, daydreaming and biding her sweet time – tick tock, tick tock. In this regard, Tommie is just like her mom. She tends to push people to their limits. Two weeks from the end of school and the start of summer vacation, Katie picked Tommie up from school and announced to her "that's all folks." No more rides. She carefully explained why. Tommie had pushed Katie's patience button one too many times.

Katie called Uranus in Iraq and informed her no more rides, period. Uranus' solution was, "she can walk to school for the remaining two weeks. The school is only about a mile or so away and a fairly safe walk." Nana Anna was quite concerned about the walking thing. Uranus called me and asked me to tell Tommie to take her cell phone with her in the morning and she would talk to her while going to and coming home from school. This would keep her safe? Go figure! Anyway, this particular brainstorm triggered multiple daily calls from Uranus to the kids, the schools, and to anyone else that would listen to her psycho babble about horrid Nana Anna and, what a terrible mistake she had made yada, yada, yada – you know the story and I won't bore you any more with it.

I must admit that I had at first agreed with Uranus about Tommie walking to school, in principle anyway. I told Uranus that I was backing up Katie, and would not give Tommie a ride. I did offer to draw out a detailed map of the safest route. Uranus wanted Tommie to walk alternate routes every day so she wouldn't be followed or picked up by the police. What was she thinking here? Did she know something I didn't know? According to Uranus, a lesson needed to be taught here. I was naïve. After all, I had walked two miles to elementary school in my day, rain or shine. But that was then. Now walking over a mile is illegal, as I quickly learned!

Booby talked to Uranus and offered to pick Tommie up and take her to/from school, but Tommie said that she would rather walk, it was OK. And walk she did, until she was spotted by a school crossing guard. The poop hit the proverbial fan (not Grope's). The incident was reported to the school by the guard and Nana Anna was notified by phone that unless Tommie was driven to school by an adult from now on, Nana Anna would be reported and charged with child neglect. Oh shit! Here we go - Booby to the rescue. Actually, the school was required by State law to report this discovery to Social Services, namely Child Protective Services. They didn't, but who's counting here. Most school administrators don't want to be bothered with reporting anything other than violence with injury. So, the school let it slide. That turned out to be a big mistake, one that came back to bite us in the butt.

But the worst part was that Uranus' frequent calls to the school became quite disturbing to me, if not out-right disgusting. Nana Anna had talked at length to the school administrator, and clearly demonstrated that she was very concerned about Tommie and guaranteed that she would be taken care of properly. Uranus, on the other hand, countered Nana Anna's discussions by ordering the school to ignore everything that Nana Anna had ever said or would say in the future, and that she, mommy dearest, was in charge from just outside Baghdad and that she was the only one to be listened to. Nana Anna was totally at fault for the incident and incompetent. Now here was the world's biggest control freak spouting off psycho babble to the schools. She was advertising to the world that Nana Anna was totally unfit to watch her kids. How is that for ignoramus logic? Did it ever enter her psychotic little mind that the schools could (should) call CPS with concern for the children's welfare? Of course NOT! Then again, how concerned are the schools anyway? They have their own set of problems. Their staff failed to recognize and/or do anything about the neglect. STRIKE 2!

The incident aside, the real problem became Uranus' frequent calls to the kids, often in secret, undermining everything that Nana Anna had been trying to do to help the children adapt, assist at home, and behave properly. Now cooperation, and even a semblance of respect for Nana Anna, would be totally impossible to obtain.

CHAPTER 20
THE VISIT

June arrived with a smile and the weather was warm and pleasant, especially nice for New Jersey. My sister-in-law Jody flew in for a week of vacation. We would spend a couple of days here in New Jersey, visit the Big Apple, and then drive to my daughter's home near the beach. You see, my daughter's family had recently been transferred to Camp LeJeune, on the East Coast.

Jody has advanced degrees in education and has worked with "special" children for over twenty years. She is brilliant and highly respected back home. I decided to ask her a favor while here. I was very concerned about Grope's behavior patterns that were being labeled as perfectly normal by Uranus. Jody agreed to help. Having been given permission from Nana Anna, we took Grope and Tommie out for ice cream, giving Jodi a short time to observe Grope. Grope exited his apartment with a big fat bionnacle in his left paw and thundered down the stairs to meet us on the sidewalk, just outside my apartment.

We could hear him slam the door on his way out. Flying downstairs, the building windows shook. Tommie arrived a minute or so later, much more reserved and polite. Walking down the street to the local Cold Stone ice cream parlor, Grope stopped and peeled gum off the sidewalk, stuck it in his mouth, and began chewing away. Then he spotted a couple of bag worms on the side bushes, snatched them up, quickly stripped off the camouflage, and began eating them too. Jodi looked on in interest. Expecting ice cream, Grope was very talkative and friendly to Jodi and continuously spouted details about his collection of bionnacle toys, the species of bugs he had captured and eaten, and how yummy they tasted with gum. On the way, we had to pull Grope back off the street, as he nearly got hit by a passing car. He had spotted more gum on the street and was paying no attention to where he was going.

After being hyper waiting in line, asking for six samples, and given his final choice of ice cream in a cup, Grope stated that he was going home to his Nana Anna, and took off like a shot before we could say a word. Tommie was well behaved the entire time and simply shook her head at Grope's bizarre behavior. Asked by Jodi if this was Grope's normal behavior, Tommie replied, "Actually he's worse most of the time." Tommie volunteered that he wiped his poop on walls, and peed all over the bathroom, and liked licking Dumpy on her private parts. If Uranus ever found out what Tommie had said to us that evening, I believe she would have tortured the poor child to death. It turned out that Jodi was not the only person she had told this to, but that came out later.

Once finished with her ice cream cup, Tommie thanked us and went bounding up the stairs to her apartment. Finally alone, I asked Jodi what she thought. Her reply was very serious. "The boy needs to be institutionalized," she said. "He is in desperate need of professional help." She asked me if I knew whether he had molested his sister, because she was pretty sure that he had or is currently doing it. His behavior sure fits the pattern. She also said, "Grope is a danger to himself and without professional help he will never be able to make it in society." Then she asked me another surprising question. "Has Grope been molested in the past? Is his mother molesting him? Poop smearing is common behavior when a child is being molested or has suffered a traumatic experience." Any Child Psychiatrist would tell you that. This stunned me. Lastly Jody said, "You should report him to Social Services and inform them that he is being left alone at home. He needs full time supervision. Anyone thinking otherwise is out of their mind or neglectful." Jodi also offered to support us and report her findings to the court if necessary. After all, she is a highly qualified professional and has many years experience with children like Grope. CPS and the Court would listen to her if they have any sense at all.

Jodi and I left for my daughters for our visit, and she flew home from there. During our visit, we had a lot of fun, forgot our worries, and I drove home two weeks later. I learned later that Jodi called Social Services about Grope. She was obliged to do so by law. Did they listen? Who knows. They did acknowledge talking to her.

CHAPTER 21
THE SHEPPARD

This Chapter is not for the weak at heart. You have been warned. "Hooray," thought Grope. "Tommie is at Surf Camp and Nana Anna is at work. I am home alone and can do whatever I want. Oh my, what to do? Oh Yeah: Here doggie, doggie." On this very day, Dumpy mysteriously started bleeding from her puppy producing parts. Dumpy had been spayed before Uranus got her, so something was wrong with the dog. By the time Nana Anna got home, blood had spread everywhere: on the beds, on the already filthy piles of clothes, on the carpet, and on the kitchen floor – everywhere. The blood was not flowing badly, but enough to require an emergency visit to the doggie doctor.

When the subject was brought up to Grope by Nana Anna, Grope said, "I didn't do anything, she just started bleeding. I was asleep in my room all day." OH YEAH!

The word about the dog spread quickly around the complex because Nana Anna announced to everyone at the pool that she had spent $200 of the child support money on the vet and a taxi. Grope, we all thought, had licked doggie too hard, poked her hoo-hoo with a pencil, his finger, a bionnacle, or something more lascivious like his wanker, you know - Mr. wiggly. The visual was just too much, too horrible for us to imagine: Grope the lonely Sheppard Boy and Dumpy, the sheep. ARRRRRGH!

Nana Anna told us a few days later that Dumpy was still

bleeding and started throwing up on the carpet. She cleaned up the mess and purchased doggy diapers. That stopped the poop, but didn't help with the vomiting. The vet supplied a big cone that prevented Dumpy from licking the wound. My immediate thoughts were, that if Grope had penetrated me in any way, I'd throw up too – a lot. I found out days later that the dog was still throwing up when I received a late afternoon phone call from Uranus. She asked me to go to the vet right away to get special food for Dumpy. Yep, Uranus started calling me from Iraq, and that meant I needed to turn off my ringer at night so I could get some sleep. I had nightmares for days afterwards, imagining Nana Anna bashing until four AM, without the Cherry Garcia and Cracker Jacks of course. Anyway, back to doggy puking. I said "sure" to Uranus, after all the vet only closed in ten minutes, and the clinic was only eight miles away. "Bye." My motorcycle is fast. I could do it. I could get there. As it turned out, it took me twenty minutes in traffic, but the vet waited for me to arrive. Uranus had called ahead.

This was good because I had a chance to talk to the vet and ask some "penetrating" questions. ICK!

"Do you know Grope?" I asked.

"Yes I do," she replied.

"Did you know he is home alone all day with Dumpy?" I asked.

"Oh God, I suspected the possibility," she said.

"In fact BRAT (Basenji Rescue and Transport) called me to discuss what might have happened. Someone had called in to them explaining the situation, and they were very suspicious." The Doctor continued, "Do you think it possible that Grope has molested the dog. Oh My God - gross!" I had no answer for her, just shook my head as I headed out the door with the food.

I wrote a sensitive email to Uranus covering the subject with as much delicacy as I could muster. She wrote back, "More

Grope bashing I see." She said that her precious boy would never do such a nasty thing. Yes, he loved tormenting the Basenji (she never called it a dog or Dumpy) but he would "NEVER" do the nasty thing with an animal. "How about with you?" I silently thought. I was immensely upset with Uranus – YA THINK!

"Take Dumpy in for a butt rub," she finally suggested. "That might help." I almost choked, holding back laughter.

Butt rub? The term remained a private joke among our small group of friends for a couple of weeks at least.

Are you tired and sore? Go get a butt rub. It fixes everything. YUK! YUK! YUK!

"My God, Uranus really is a Psycho," someone said. "No, she's just a Bitch," someone else said. The name stuck. From there on out "Psycho Bitch" became the operative name for Uranus. Psycho Bitch – there is a pleasant and truthful ring to it.

Anyway, Dumpy's bleeding continued non-stop for two months or longer – even after... Ooops that is getting ahead again. Hint! I'll tell you the truth for a dime – YACK! Think about it!

CHAPTER 22
POOL TIME

S ummer was moving along at an amazing pace. Tommie arrived back from "Surf Camp" with a nice tan from the southern beaches. I was jealous. I had wanted to go see my daughter and grandsons again, and spend some more time on the beach. Tommie had enjoyed her time surfing the same North Carolina beaches I will go to when I eventually get to see my daughter and grandsons again.

That's OK though, because we have a really nice pool at the apartment, and the weather was finally getting to the point where a day at the pool was possible without rain – well most of the time. Summer in this part of New Jersey can be stifling. Kids under 14 are not allowed in the pool without a parent or guardian. The age had been raised by building management because of Grope. It used to be 13. Grope was now 13 going on 7. He could be a real menace if not supervised, and he wasn't.

Grope loved the pool when he was not tormenting Dumpy, sucking out brains, or doing whatever he did alone upstairs. He especially loved the pool when there were lots of bugs to harvest and eat from the surrounding bushes. Yep! Bag worms were now plentiful and hanging on the shrubs outside the pool fence, and he could pick them at will, strip off the camouflage, and suck on the wiggly worms. Then chew them up saying to whoever would listen, "yummy, snacks."

On nice days, Nana Anna would bring the kids to the pool

after she got home from work in the late afternoon. She would carry down a plate of marinated chicken to barbeque for their dinner. Often times we were already there, and she would join us to chat while her food was cooking. We were all becoming fast friends.

During the week, we felt so bad for Tommie and Grope. When Nana Anna was at work, they would walk around the pool in agony. Sometimes, more often than not, we would invite Tommie and Grope to the pool to join us, and all the kids would play in the water. Katie's kids, and others at the pool, got along great with Tommie, and everyone had fun. Tommie was never a problem. I would play silly water games with them like monkey in the middle. Then I would throw a football in the air and they would jump in from the edge and try to catch the ball before going under water. We would also play skimmer ball, where we skipped a soft rubber ball across the pool and would get points if we could stick the ball into the skimmer. Dumb, yes. Fun, absolutely. Value: Priceless. The kids were great and would never tire from the games. Even the lifeguard joined in the fun.

I missed my grandchildren so very much, so, aside from the fun, these games eased my withdrawals from not seeing them as often as I would like.

At times, Grope played with us too, but he would usually catch the ball and want everyone to chase him around the pool and the deck to get it back, and then, just before he was captured, he would throw the ball over the pool fence. HA, HA, HA – so much fun – NOT! Keep in mind, Grope never went to the pool without a big fat bionnacle in his paw. He would swim with it and scratch the backs of other swimmers saying, "It's going to eat you." Yes, he even stuck wiggly bag worms into the mouth of his "Alien Queen" toy sent by his mom and wanted everyone to look and see the guts flow. Come to think of it, now I know why the pool was never very crowded when he was there.

ICK! YUK! BUGS! - ICK! YUK! Grope! This was truly sad.

I am appearing quite mean here. In reality, I care for Grope very much. He is a really good kid, just big-time socially retarded. He has so many mental problems. Being Autistic with Asperger's' Syndrome, Grope is very hard to deal with most of the time. Asperger's' Syndrome kids are often brilliant, but usually socially retarded. That definition fits Grope like a glove. Often times he sulks and wanders back to his room. Grope really needs professional help, but I am beating that fact to death. We all knew the issues, but Uranus just refused to see it. She was in total denial about his behavior, even though she knew he had the Syndrome. At some point, one of us would need to take the steps to make it happen, regardless of the consequences.

Pool time was a great chance to chat while the kids played. It was there that Katie and I met a very charming young lady named Cherry. Cherry just recently married a local tennis pro, and moved here in our complex. She is intelligent and very mature for her young age. We quickly became friends. We learned that Cherry often invited her fourteen year-old niece Melanie to stay with her for days at a time. Tommie and Melanie had met a week or so earlier and become fast friends. Soon Tommie was spending nights with Melanie, Cherry, and her husband, Martin. Tommie was very happy for the first time in a long time. I believed it had a lot to do with experiencing normalcy. Cherry and Melanie were great for Tommie. This was her escape from her lonely, miserable, motherless, home life. The sad part, though, was that Grope now stayed home, alone most of the time.

CHAPTER 23
NOT AT THIS SCHOOL, YOU WON'T

Summer was waning and back-to-school days were approaching. Grope was returning to the same school, so there was no issue there. Tommie, on the other hand, was to transfer to a middle school about the same distance from the apartment complex, but in the opposite direction. Katie, finally having signed and notarized Power of Attorney authorization papers from Uranus, offered to take the paperwork to the school and register Tommie. An upcoming half-day orientation had been announced by mail. All the local children were excited about the session and Tommie was no exception, but she had to be registered to attend.

Katie arrived at the school office and handed the papers that Nana Anna had prepared to the administrative assistant. This resulted in a blank stare from her.

"Are you the mother," she asked?

"No," Katie replied.

"Are you the legal guardian?"

"No."

"Then you can't do this. Only a parent can or a legal guardian can register a child." The lady was nice about it but seemed cold and very firm.

"I have a signed power of attorney from the mother allowing me to do just that," stated Katie as she handed her the paper.

Tossing the paper back to Katie, she rudely said "That paper is worthless here. I remember Uranus, and I specifically told her that she needed a **signed** court order specifying legal guardianship. The Guardian must show the proper papers and only then will I register Tommie." She was as getting quite huffy.

Katie explained the situation again, and asked to see her supervisor. The lady maintained her cold position and said, "I am in charge. There is no one else here." The woman's behavior was pure insolence, PMS personified.

I remember that Uranus and I had gone to the school before she left for Iraq and we had made all of the arrangements for Tommie's transfer. In fact, we had met with the same woman and she had made no such statement to us at that time. She was lying for some reason. This woman was feeding Katie a bunch of hooey, but there was no point in going further, because the nasty woman was adamant and the so-called "person in charge." In closing, the woman suggested that Katie read the Regulations for Seaford County. Then she added, "The legal Guardian must also take a residency class and provide proper paperwork to get the transfer done." Katie left the school in an uproar. Don't you love the system? You've got to love it. The woman was an outright imbecile. I knew she was blowing smoke.

When Katie called me and explained the problem, I wrote an email to Uranus stating the situation, telling her that I would be checking into this in more detail, but that she should consider the possibility of coming home to get her daughter registered, just in case. This did not sit well with Uranus, but she caved in and said that she would put in for leave, since her four month vacation was coming up. She told me that she was planning on vacationing in Viet Nam, but would come home if absolutely necessary.

I called the Seaford County Department of Social Services to find out the rules about custody and guardianship regulations. My research paid off, uncovering that no "formal" paperwork is required for a single parent to go to Iraq, as long as she has the children being cared for by "someone," a "caretaker." This fact actually alarmed me somewhat. Anyone could watch the kids? Oh my!

Then I called the Seaford County Department of Education and was told that, just as I had suspected, Katie had been fed a bunch of crap by the so-called administrator. Registering the child should be no problem at all for Nana Anna and no special residential training program was required.

Uranus called me later asking about the status, and I told her that the heat was off, and that Nana Anna could do the job herself. In fact, we learned later, even Katie could have registered Tommie for her with a note and a copy of the apartment lease. We wondered why all of the trouble was given to us at the school. Perhaps Uranus' or Nana Anna's reputation had migrated from the other school. Who knows? Regardless, the pressure was off of Uranus, forcing her to travel home, and she knew it. I followed up with emails to Uranus confirming my findings. After all, she had a habit of conveniently forgetting conversations through "selective hearing." I personally thought selective hearing was a male disease, having been told that by my past wife several times. Go figure. Maybe Uranus had some male genes.

Middle school orientation day was approaching fast, and Uranus had already put in for a leave request for home, or so we were told. She also sent us emails saying that she was coming home and would register Tommie herself - period. We were to do nothing more. So we let the matter go. That was a mistake on our part.

CHAPTER 24
THE LAST STRAW

All conversations with Uranus, by email or by phone resulted in different excuses and stories as to how and when she was coming home. She even said that she would register Tommie in school at some point later because she was planning to take off with the kids for Mississippi to visit her fireman boyfriend when she arrived home. Her boyfriend had quit his job and returned from Iraq. Yes, Uranus was not-so-secretly having unauthorized sex with someone in Iraq on a regular basis. This could have resulted in termination of her job if she had been caught, but she was obviously too horny to care about that. Remember her absolute defiance to rules of any kind. No rules applied to her at any level.

As far as Uranus was concerned, Tommie could miss the orientation and start school late. Uranus had already called the school. A former Marine and student advisor at the new school would gladly show Tommie around when she eventually got back from Mississippi, if she ever got back, driving her broken down car, still without a license and insurance. Uranus's id was raging again and my tolerance and patience limit with her had finally boiled over.

In truth, I figured that Uranus had no intention of coming back to the USA. She was heading for Viet Nam for a vacation with an Army girlfriend. She would tell us later, at the very last minute. I had guessed, and found out I was totally correct after she arrived home by force. That part of the story comes up shortly. In fact, let's go there now.

CHAPTER 25
WE DID IT

*"We do not have to visit a madhouse to find disordered minds;
our planet is the mental institution of the universe"*
- Johann von Goethe

W e had all talked about it ever since Uranus left for Iraq. We all knew that morally and legally we should do it, but were reluctant because we had all been friends with Uranus and were friends with Nana Anna. Nana Anna would probably catch most of the blame and unjustly so. Uranus had dropped bombs on her and left her standing in the cold, bleeding. Uranus had bailed out knowing full well that Nana Anna could not possibly take care of the children. She knew Nana Anna was a terrible housekeeper. The only one she had thought of was herself, and her immediate escape to Iraq to have fun, have sex with her boyfriend in Camp Fallujah, escape responsibility, make big bucks, and blow it all on trinkets.

Nana Anna was stuck in a part time, dead-end job. I had offered her the use of my spare computer and training software to practice up on her Microsoft Office skills so she could find a reasonable paying job and move home. Her mother was dying and her real family missed her. They wanted her home. She wanted to go home, too. Uranus wasn't even blood related, but Nana Anna cared for her even though she was used and abused by her. Nana Anna also loved the kids, despite their total lack of respect, and their refusal to help her in any way. She knew their attitude came directly from Uranus through history and through her daily phone calls. Uranus was a pathetically selfish woman. Nana Anna realized that as fact.

Nana Anna accepted my offer for the computer. For a few days, she practiced on it in my apartment to ensure it was running properly. Katie's husband and I took my computer and a spare long table upstairs to her apartment. This was the first time I had entered the place since Uranus had bailed out to Iraq. Because of Katie's and Cherry's continued help, most of the house was cleaned by now. Katie and Cherry had helped because we all expected Uranus home any day. Yes, Nana Anna was terrified of Uranus. Hell, we all were. The house still looked like it had been decorated ghetto style, but the carpet where the computer table was placed had been scrubbed clean (I think with bleach and whatever else worked). The stink was less noticeable, but still there, and a pile of clothes four feet wide and two feet deep remained in the hall with blood and other stuff caked on them (don't ask). Grope's room still smelled like the Penn Station subway stairway and I refused to look in it or go upstairs to where Nana Anna spent a lot of time, but the smell rolled down the stairs like a clammy fog. We set up the table, the computer, and the software, fired it up to verify everything worked, and left. I stripped and took a hot shower when I got home. So did Katie's husband.

Before the big announcement, let's recap for a minute. Tommie was staying away as much as possible with Melanie at Cherry's house. Tommie wasn't registered at school, and the orientation was only days away. Nana Anna was still working and being mistreated by the kids and tormented by Uranus. The kids were lying to Uranus on a daily basis, telling her exactly what she wanted to hear. Dumpy was still peeing, pooping, and bleeding all over everything, but the pee pads did help some. The house, although cleaner, still reeked. The carpet was stained beyond recognition and Grope was still Grope – home alone with bleeding doggie most of the time doing whatever he wanted to do. Does that do it?

It did it for me and Katie. Fully recognizing that Uranus is insane and dead set on satisfying only her own needs and screw everyone else, I called Child Protective Services. Then I then made a walk-in appointment with them. This horror could go on no longer. The kids needed to be taken care of. Grope needed a special fulltime home, perhaps an institution, plus intensive therapy. Tommie needed deprogramming and a lot of TLC from loving Foster parents. Nana Anna needed to go home. The apartment needed to be burned to the ground. Lastly, Uranus needed to have her ovaries removed and the kids taken from her permanently without visitation rights and then sent away, placed in the center of an Iraqi mine field without a bomb map. Yeah: That about does it.

Katie decided to go with me. I was happy for the support. We walked into the building together, prepared to start a war, one that would last for a long time.

CHAPTER 26
THE FIRST CPS MEETING

O ur first visit to CPS resulted in our meeting with Ms. Cortez, a mid-thirties Social Worker who could barely speak English. We greeted her and she said, "Ningún favor inglés capaz del poro." Whatever that means! We spent over an hour speaking with her, repeating ourselves several times and speaking slowly, and using hand gestures. She appeared to be taking copious notes - or scribbles. I am not sure if she was writing or doodling on her note pad. I assumed correctly that she only understood a small amount of what we told her. Mostly she shook her head yes and muttered "I see" or was it "Ah Si?" We should have read the notes taken or brought in an interpreter from El Salvador. OH MY! Follow-up meetings with others clarified that many points we made were not recorded properly.

The verbal report we initially gave was detailed and filled with the horrors we all had encountered since Uranus moved in late last year. We were told by Ms. Cortez in broken English, that Uranus had a long and distinguished record [of child abuse] and we had done the right thing coming in. We would be asked to support them in court, should there be a trial, and we would be subpoenaed for attendance along with a request for any documentation we could provide. Actually, I believe we were asked for that later by another Social Worker, I am not quite sure. Regardless, we both had a ton of paper to offer. Uranus' ranting and raving emails filled terra bytes of disk space, well, megabytes is more like it. Her typing speed was faster than her mind so her sordid confessions were long, detailed, and candid to the point of melting candle wax if exposed to the air.

We had specifically asked that Nana Anna, albeit a lousy house cleaner, not be charged because she was not totally at fault here. Before Uranus left for Iraq, Nana Anna was very forward and admitted that she was still a slob, but Uranus didn't care. She just wanted out. Uranus was the criminal here, not Nana Anna. CPS agreed to be kind to Nana Anna. But Uranus and her sleazy criminal lawyer changed all that in court.

CHAPTER 27
BYE BYE KIDDIES

Social Services Child Protective Services (CPS) wanted Uranus' ass some kind of bad. They were still at the plate and the count was strike 2. They had the balls to swing away! This time they needed a hit to score; and a score is what they were after. CPS wasted no time. As I walked out of my apartment the next morning, I spotted Grope with a sad frown on his face, shuffling along near my mailbox. He was hunched over, carrying a backpack filled with bionnacle toys, and a big one in his left paw. There were tears in his eyes. I walked up and hugged him, asking the boy what the problem was? He said, "Two ladies came to the door with papers and came in the house with a camera and took pictures." I know for fact that both of the kids and Nana Anna had been told by Guido to let no one in the house - ever, even with a warrant, until he was able to get there. Ooops! Grope let them in. Go ladies, go! Grope whispered that they were now walking over to Cherry's apartment to talk to Tommie. Yes! Grope had been left all alone at home again – a big no-no! I felt so sad for him, but hopeful that he would soon be in better hands.

An hour later, I learned from Katie that she had received a call from Cherry. CPS had visited her apartment and talked to Tommie on the walkway outside her door. The Social Workers left with both the children, and they were now at the crisis center downtown, soon to be placed into Foster care. We later heard from one of the Social Workers that the Office of Health and Human Services intended to file for permanent removal of the kids. As luck would have it, the apartment was a sewer again, and this time they had a warrant and the pictures to prove that the conditions the children were living under were intolerable. You see, Grope had fed Dumpy a bunch of chicken and chicken bones during the night, after being strictly told by Nana Anna not to do so. Dumpy had deposited vomit and diarrhea puddles all over the house. The apartment looked much like it did before Katie and Cherry cleaned it. Good for Grope, I thought! Maybe there is justice after all! You know the saying "skill will out?" Mine is now and forever "poop will out!" Out go the kids, that is. It was about time. God Bless CPS. God Bless the kids.

CHAPTER 28
COME HOME URANUS, YOUR KIDS HAVE BEEN TAKEN

I thought the nightmare was about over, and the children would finally be cared for properly, but the real horror was just beginning. As I said in the last chapter, I was told by Katie that the kids had been taken by Child Protective Services. Of course, Nana Anna had been notified, and she was on her way home. She totally freaked out and all she could say was "I will be held at fault."

I thought it best to call Uranus myself because she had avoided talking to Katie for a long time now and she barely knew Cherry, albeit predictably, she told Cherry her entire life story the first time she talked to her on the phone. It was all Cherry could do to keep from getting sick before hanging up. "Who is this maniac?" asked Cherry when she spoke to Katie a while later. I was, for the moment, still on Uranus' good guy list, only because I needed to keep current with her activities for the kids' sake. I had been playing her, I admit it. I knew her trust wouldn't last. But the call would surely light a fire under her derrière and initiate her flight home. I got through to her and she was alarmed with the news, but not overly surprised – go figure. At this point she must have assumed the visit by the Social Workers was one of their periodic checks from the last neglect court episode with them, and, of course, they had found Grope home alone with the house a total pig sty. She knew about the apartment. She had Tommie's pictures. Uranus told me that she would try to get emergency leave from KBR and come home right away. Note the fact that she had NOT yet arranged for "leave" to come home and register Tommie in school.

Well, Uranus arrived in Baghdad by helicopter within an hour or two after my call. Isn't it funny how fast one can move when prodded the appropriate way? Yes, it was obvious to all of us that she no intention to come home and register Tommie in school. As for getting home right away, that is not exactly how it all happened.

While in Baghdad, Uranus called and actually talked to Katie (surprise of surprises). Uranus told Katie she was in Baghdad and would be on a flight to Dubai within three hours. Just minutes later on the same call, I talked to her, and Uranus told me that she had no tickets yet, but hoped to get out by tomorrow or the next day. Remember the "telephone game?" What could we believe? Three hours or a week! Was she lying or was she officially loosing it - probably a little of both. Let's give her a little leeway here, and just say that her mind was playing games with her.

As luck would have it, the timing was terrible. I was planning to leave for my daughter's home the next morning for a visit and a chance to bask in the warm North Carolina sun on Onslow Beach before it got too cold. I had also invited Katie and her kids to go with me. Katie's son is my youngest grandson's best friend, and they missed each other after being apart for some time now. This was a perfect chance for them to see each other again.

At 2 AM, I received a phone call. I had forgotten to turn off the ringer. Groping for the phone, I placed the receiver to my ear and heard a squeaky voice say: "Are you awake yet? I thought you might be up because I know you are leaving early in the morning. I am still in Baghdad and don't have a flight out yet. KBR is giving me leave without pay, and I need you to call the Red Cross to try and get me an emergency flight – they might even pay for it."

OK, so what she had told me about her departure earlier was somewhat more on target. Why she told Katie what she did was a bit confusing. Then I thought that Uranus' lie was probably said to scare the hell out of Nana Anna. She is fully aware that Katie and Nana Anna talk a lot. Regardless, feeling sorry for her, primarily because I initiated this mess, I said. "OK, I'll call!" I got up, looked up the local Red Cross 24 hour emergency number on the internet, and made a call. I explained the situation to a new, but sympathetic Red Cross employee. The young man said he would take care of it. He would put an immediate call into his supervisor and get the ball moving. I gave him the information and the number in Baghdad to call, a KBR security number at which he could reach Uranus. I hung up, leaving the rest to them. Before hanging up, the Red Cross agent gave me a case number for reference. I called the same number in Baghdad that I had given the agent, and told the security person on duty that I had set the ball in motion with the Red Cross. I gave them the Red Cross case number and asked them to tell Uranus. The Security Guard called out the information to Uranus, sitting not too far from the phone. I had done all I could do for now, so I went back to bed to try and catch a little more sleep before getting up. Impossible!

As it turned out, Uranus was incorrect in her assumption about my departure time. We were actually going to leave around noon, but because Nana Anna was so upset and thinking that CPS was after only her, we decided to delay the trip one more day and stay with Nana Anna, trying to comfort her as best we could. She was frantic about what Uranus would do to her if she saw the apartment like it was. I was worried about her heart. I don't blame her because the apartment was, indeed, a cesspool again.

Nana Anna planned to go on a cleaning frenzy and asked for our help. I advised against it because we wanted the courts to see what they should see. I know this sounds mean, but the filthy house was one of the key reasons CPS took the kids in the first place. It wouldn't help our case to clean it for her. We advised Nana Anna to leave the mess for Uranus, but Nana Anna would not hear of it. It was obvious that she was terrified; saying that Uranus and the Court would blame her for everything. As it turned out, Nana Anna was definitely right on that point. Uranus blamed everything on her alone – for the moment.

Katie, her kids, and I left the following day at noon for my daughters home in North Carolina. Unfortunately, we had to return a few days later, cutting the vacation short. The reasons for the quick return will become clear in what happened next.

CHAPTER 29
HERE COMES THE JUDGE

We were at my daughter's house on the day the first CPS hearing was held, days just after the children had been removed from the apartment and placed into Foster Care. Shortly before court convened, Katie received a call from a male lawyer claiming to be the Attorney representing Child Protective Services. He asked her a series of strange questions, primarily why she would NOT want the children to return home to Uranus immediately. Katie was a bit flustered at the question and gave the first negative response that came to mind. The lawyer quickly said he had to hang up because the Judge was calling them all into to the court room. The call seemed really funny to us. In the first place, why didn't the lawyer ask me any questions? After all, we both were working with the Department of Social Services and both were key contacts. We now believe in retrospect that the call really came from the scumbag Guido. The sneaky bastard was feeling out Katie and how she felt, thinking it may be possible to use her testimony in court to help his insane client. WRONG! Why didn't he speak to me? Simple, I say. I would have recognized Guido's voice immediately, having seen and spoken with him a number of times. This misrepresentation by Guido was criminal in our minds. We were fairly sure it had to be him because we knew of no male lawyers on this case at Social Services. It just had to have been Guido. What a slimy bastard! Hmmm, how did he know about Katie in the first place, and how did he get her number? Of course, Uranus gave it to him, and Uranus still thought I was on her side. Was it a fishing expedition? You bet it was.

Yep! Court was in session. Uranus was still sitting on her boney butt in a chair in Baghdad trying to get home. Regardless, the initial hearing resulted in a disaster for Child Protective Services. Nana Anna went to the hearing totally against our advice. She had not been subpoenaed. We begged her to stay away. She simply would not listen. You guessed it. Guido called her to the stand and ripped her to shreds, blaming everything on her. He also openly lied to the Court about a number of things, and what made matters worse, there were no objections made by Nana Anna. She was too petrified to speak up. He claimed to the Court that Nana Anna was entirely responsible and poor Uranus was just an innocent victim, dedicating her time in Iraq, putting her life in harms way, serving her country while all this madness was taking place. **Hey – the military serves, she was there to serve herself and service other male residents of Camp Fallujah.** She left the country fully aware that this could happen; that this would eventually happen. It just erupted sooner than she expected. Guido continued distorting the facts by claiming the poop on the walls, as shown in the pictures taken by Child Protective Services, was only dog poop. Do we need a lab test here? How did the dog poop get six feet up the wall? How did it smear and stick? Lastly, Guido said the apartment was now acceptably clean, thanks to "friends" like Cherry who came over and cleaned up the entire mess for Nana Anna. This part was true, and I couldn't say I told you so. Cherry is too caring. Much to the chagrin of CPS, the whole hearing caved in like an unstable house of cards.

Court was dismissed. We did not receive the results from Social Services but heard directly from Cherry and Nana Anna that the kids were, indeed, going home to Uranus at some point, and that Nana Anna was banned from watching the kids for life. Guido walked out of the courtroom, his chest all puffy. He was extremely pleased with his self accomplishments. He had cleaned up the floor with Nana Anna, the inept CPS lawyer and the stupid Social Workers. His golfing buddy, Judge Dread, had refused to hear testimony from anyone other than Nana Anna. Cherry had been there to describe the horrid mess, the persecution of Nana Anna by Uranus, and to raise the fact that Grope had been left alone most of the summer, contrary to court requirements. Katie and I, as well as Cherry, were fit to be tied. Nana Anna was petrified. STRIKE 3!

Katie and I were on the road home from my daughters, defeated and miserable. Cherry called and told us that a second hearing will be held shortly after Uranus arrives home from Iraq. Guido had stated that he felt that the whole thing was a slam dunk and told that to Uranus by phone, but the fat lady had not yet sung and that thought cheered us up a bit – just a small bit. Guido had won a battle but certainly not the war.

CHAPTER 30
THE ARRIVAL

Not a bad movie, a bit of a reach, but not bad. Charlie Sheen has done better. However, Uranus' "arrival" home was another story altogether and would make a great horror movie. It took three days for her to get home from Baghdad. After the long wait and endless flight, she had to take the Airport Bus home because no one would pick her up. She was tired and raging mad. Uranus stormed upstairs, blew into the apartment, and began ripping on Nana Anna. The walls rumbled. "This whole damned mess is entirely your fault," she screamed. "You are such a fracking slob, it's no wonder they took the kids. This cost me money I don't have, and you ruined up my vacation plans in Viet Nam."

Now don't forget that the apartment had just been "re-cleaned" by Nana Anna and Cherry. It looked much better than the smelly cauldron it had been and much better than Uranus had ever cleaned anything in her life. Of course, the paint on Grope's walls had been stripped bare in places from scraping off his poop and some of the carpet had been bleached white. Caked-in poop and other ground in crud can do that when cleaned with Clorox mixed with Lysol and carpet cleaner – gallons of it. We were all sure that Grope's jungle still smelled putrid, but all in all, the place looked much better.

CHAPTER 31
HERE COMES THE JUDGE

Immediately after Uranus arrived home, a second hearing was quickly arranged with Judge Dread, Guido, Uranus, Child Protective Services, and another of their contract lawyers. Unprepared again, this session went somewhat poorly, in fact as bad as the first one. Guido was on a roll and the CPS lawyer again appeared to be powerless, having absolutely no voice and apparently totally deaf to what was being said. Guido ripped the lady lawyer into shreds. The Social Workers left the court heads down, and in tears. Yes, the kids were on their way home to Uranus. Guido was all puffy because he was having his way.

Judge Dread repeated that Nana Anna was no longer allowed to watch the kids – ever again! Grope and Tommie were to remain in custody until the apartment was totally clean and inspected by CPS. The fact that Nana Anna could no longer watch the children made her sad, but it was truly best for her health. We all knew that. Now, if she could survive Uranus' wrath; if we could get her cross trained and assist her in finding a job back home, she could go home to her real family – the family that wanted her and truly cared for her.

Hang on readers, I repeat: the fat lady has not yet sung and this is just the beginning of a never ending story. Another hearing was scheduled and held without Judge Dread presiding. Guido was quite upset about that. He tried to alter the date, but failed. The Judge du jour was more tuned into CPS and ordered yet another hearing to review a detailed 24/7 child-care plan to be prepared by Uranus, the crazy woman herself. The Judge stated that if the plan was not accepted by the court, complete with background checks of the child care participants, Uranus could not return to Iraq, and if she did, she would lose her kids permanently. A hint of daylight was peeking through the dense fog and clouds. Guido was embarrassed and livid at the same time. In fact, the Judge put Guido in his place a number of times and queried him as to why he was working out of his field of criminal law and defending Uranus. The Judge said that Guido should leave Juvenile Court issues to the experts.

CHAPTER 32
KIDDIES, COME HOME TO MOMMY

After the second hearing, the kids were still in custody of the court, but shamefully would be returned to Uranus the same day because Feather announced to the court before the Judge left that the apartment had already been inspected and passed with flying colors. Yes, the apartment was clean.

A Social Worker friend told us that Tommie cried when she was picked up at her Foster home. She did not want to return home because she loved her Foster home, and was being well taken care of for once in her life. This made both the Social Worker and the Foster parents very sad. Grope, on the other hand, appeared to be totally indifferent and perhaps even happy to be going home. There was good reason for that. Grope had been placed in a State institution for special children, basically a nearby mental institution. When picked up, he was filthy dirty, and wore the same smelly clothes that he had on when he had left home several days before. The Child Placement system is certainly not perfect, and Grope's treatment is a prime example of that. Not only was he filthy, but he also had an untreated scratch on his arm; the result of an attack from another mentally ill child in the facility. The information about Grope's injury was offered by Uranus when she confronted me in the entryway to our apartment building the day after the hearing. I say confronted because, by now, she suspected I had been involved with the "kidnapping" of her children by those "Orwellian Nazi's," as she put it. I am sure the term came from Guido. The chance of Uranus having ever read George Orwell's 1984 is remote. Well, maybe not that remote. She does love to read about world religions, and I did see copies of The Manchurian Candidate, Mein Kampf, and Animal Farm in her apartment long ago. I also saw a book entitled "Mind Control Made Easy." Go figure!

I also learned from Nana Anna that Tommie had been given new clothes by her Foster Parents, and arrived home very clean, well groomed, and well taken care of in every way. No wonder she wanted to stay – normalcy again. Of course, Uranus threw out the new clothes from the Foster parents, and all of the other clothes Nana Anna had bought her while she was in Iraq.

Later on that day, I ran into Nana Anna outside the Apartment Complex, and she told me in confidence that the kids greeted their mother very timidly, in fact somewhat coldly. Grope immediately asked mom if she would buy him an Alien costume as a present. He had seen it on EBay and it only cost three thousand dollars. Hearing this, Uranus blew a fuse. "I just spent four thousand dollars getting here and I had to give up my fracking vacation in Viet Nam – so shut up about presents. There will be no damn presents for anyone."

This Kodak moment did not go over well with the kids. Uranus was just getting started and ordered Nana Anna to go to her half-room and to stay put. "You can stay with us for now, but you must remain in your room. That's it. Go out to eat, stay away from my kids, don't you dare talk to them, and keep out of my face," she commanded. "I am paying the bills here and I am in charge now."

YEAH! And you're still bouncing checks too – you miserable slut!

After the arrival pleasantries were finished, Uranus took

Dumpy and Tommie out for a long doggie walk, to pee, and poop - the dog, not Tommie. I'm not so sure about Uranus; you know, Iraq is primitive in many ways. While Uranus was away from the apartment, Nana Anna called Katie and wanted a shoulder to cry on. She was terrified. Katie called me and we all met across the street at a local curb-side fast food place, and spent the next several hours talking to her and trying to calm her down. Uranus had literally gone postal. And, with Uranus and Tommie out and Nana Anna with us, Grope was home alone again, despite the court order.

In my mind Uranus had now become the perfect poster model for "Mommy Dearest" – you know - Joan Crawford reincarnated. From then on out, Nana Anna had to check in with "Mommy Dearest" to get permission to use the pool pass, to use the bathroom, to talk, to use the phone, and to enter or leave the apartment. The situation was really sad, but we all, including Nana Anna, got a good laugh. Why not? Laughing at Uranus was certainly better than maiming her, and laughing is legal and a hell of a lot safer. Uranus had truly lost her marbles while in Neverland, the whole damn bag.

Now the kids were being coached to fear us, and to no longer talk to any of us. In fact, Uranus told Cherry, unsuspected as a conspirator at this point, that her lawyer Guido had found out that both Kate and I were the backstabbing traitors that reported her. Of course it was true, but there is no lawful way that Guido could know anything. Uranus had to be on a fishing expedition, or was she? Had Guido broken the law? He is very slimy. Had Feather at CPS told him? I didn't trust her. Did he have someone else inside CPS?

Over the next several days, Uranus cleaned her house, including having the carpets professionally steam cleaned. That didn't help too much; the kid's rooms were trashed again within days, but that didn't seem to matter to Uranus. Their rooms were their problem. Nana Anna, having been allocated a tiny, half closet in the apartment to store all of her possessions, had been forced to place several of her clothes in the downstairs hall closet while Uranus was away. These items were yanked out of the closet by Uranus. Many of her clothing items were thrown into the dumpster across the street, with an after the fact explanation by Uranus that "you have too damn many clothes and don't need them all." The rest of her clothes and goods were thrown on her half of the bedroom floor and her small bed. "Deal with it or get out," she said, dark eyed and threatening.

CHAPTER 33
REDECORATING THE DEN OF INIQUITY

Remember that I said I had loaned my computer system and long table to Nana Anna so she could improve her office skills and find a better job? Uranus, being totally inconsistent with her desire to lose Nana Anna, ordered the immediate removal of the computer. Katie and I reluctantly brought the equipment back to my apartment when Uranus was not home. While inside her home gathering up the computer, we noticed that the house looked cleaner, but Grope's room still smelled horrid, and the stairs leading to Uranus's private rooms upstairs reeked of dog urine - or Gropes' or Uranus,' who can be sure.

Once the computer was removed, Uranus took the table I had loaned Nana Anna, and placed it outside her apartment against the wall. Katie's husband picked it up later and took it to my garage. Then Uranus placed ugly, stained mattresses along the dining room window where the table had been located. Then she covered the mattresses with flowered sheets. The moldy mattresses were to serve as floor couches or whatever. The apartment took on the appearance of a whore house, with enough mattresses for large group sex parties. Of course, mid-eastern motif was her style, her karma, so I assume the arrangement was appropriate for that sort of thing, at least for Uranus.

Dumpy loved the change, because she had lots of comfy

places to sleep, poop, pee, and bleed; and there were windows so she could look outside by standing on the mattresses and stinky throw pillows.

Keep in mind that Uranus threw out the many pee pads that Nana Anna had strategically installed in the apartment to protect the carpets and floors. Uranus was furious that Nana Anna had bought them to begin with. Remember, she had told Nana Anna to remove them and walk Dumpy more often. I must be honest here. The dog was being walked a lot more now since Uranus was home; and she was dragging Tommie with her. These walks were about the only time Tommie was allowed outside. Grope was still being left alone in the house, despite the court order. We never saw him.

OK, I have beat to death the fact that Uranus' has total disdain for the law; total disrespect for authority, and rules of any kind. We understood the Judge had ordered supervision for Grope at all times, but he could just stick it as far as Uranus was concerned. She knew what was best for her children and no one else knew squat.

CHAPTER 34
LET THE BRAINWASHING BEGIN

"Just as most soldiers believe bullets will hit only others, not themselves, most citizens like to think that their own minds and thought processes are invulnerable."

Margaret Singer, Ph.D.

Tommie and Grope were not the happiest kids to see their mom return from Iraq. Nana Anna kept us appraised of their condition. From a distance, we could see sadness in Tommie's face, and knew the kids were miserable.

Uranus knew about mind control. It was difficult to determine just how controlling Uranus had become. But it was obvious that she had become successful through her actions. She had definitely watched the old Manchurian Candidate movie a number of times and read the book. At first we wondered why the kids would not talk to us or even look at us. We learned from Nana Anna that Uranus prohibited the children from speaking or even looking at any one of us. When on the street with Uranus, Tommie would look over at us with yearning in her eyes, but Uranus would always grab her and snap her head straight forward, then whisper something nasty to her. Rarely did we see Grope. When we did, he always shuffled along behind Tommie, head pointed downward. We could see that Uranus was concentrating hard on training Tommie first. Nana Anna told us that Uranus would not let

Tommie out of her sight 24/7. She kept her isolated at home, and even made her sleep with her, to ensure she could not speak with Nana Anna or sneak outside. Or was it possible that she was isolating her from Grope? Nana Anna also said that Uranus constantly reminded the children that Katie and I were evil. She was applying all of the brainwashing techniques she could think of or had read in Mind Control Made Easy. And as I already mentioned, her techniques were apparently working.

What Uranus didn't know was that the kids had already explained a lot to Child Protective Services, and CPS was preparing to drop a nuclear bomb on her, or so we hoped.

CHAPTER 35
ROLLING, ROLLING, ROLLING · SPLAT!

Knock, knock! "Who's there?"
Sound familiar? It was very early in the morning, the sun just peeking above the horizon. Of course the door knocker was Uranus. Who else could it be? I dressed quickly and opened the door.

"I need my car papers!" she stated with beady eyes and a not-so-friendly look on her pasty white face.

Sleepily, I replied: "I think I gave them back to Nana Anna, but I will look around."

"I need then NOW," she demanded! "I need to go to MVA and get my tags this morning."

I mean, like poof, here they are! Screw you, bitch. Could I pull the papers out of thin air? I hadn't been involved with the car for a long while now, ever since I turned the problem with Baldy at MVA back to Uranus and Guido to handle. Now that she was home, the car became a big priority. Here is Uranus with a major attitude, straight and true to the core. What was Ms Dracula doing out in the daylight? Go back to your coffin and I will look.

For the next two hours, I tore through all of my boxes of papers and receipts that I keep in my apartment. My apartment was quickly becoming a paper quagmire. Yep! I'm a paper pack rat. What writer isn't? I couldn't "find" the paperwork. I was irritated, missing my morning dream session, my coffee, and I was convinced the papers were not in my apartment. Eventually, after my apartment became totally trashed with paper, a light bulb went off in my head. Ooops! Had I placed the papers in a very safe place, like in my armoire? If you ever want to hide something permanently, place it in your armoire.

We've all been there, I hope anyway. I don't think I am alone in misplacing important stuff. Safe place, my ass! Hidden to the max in the most unlikely place is more like it! Anyway, I had struck pay dirt; I found the envelope tucked safely in the top cabinet of my armoire. I felt a sheepish look form on my face. Dementia had certainly set in. I am getting old, I told myself. I picked up the envelope clearly marked "CAR" in my hands, and called Uranus on her (Nana Anna's) phone, mildly apologized, and told her that I had found the papers. She sent Tommie to fetch them immediately. But being a masochist and filled with curiosity, I wanted her to make sure everything was in order, so I followed Tommie to the Apartment Building Computer Center, where Uranus was madly typing out something on the computer. Could it be a plan? Of course it could! Or maybe not! Could it be "chat?" Nah! It had to be a plan. She checked the papers and casually dismissed me with a wave of her hand, without saying a word.

It was then I mentioned that Nana Anna had virtually told everyone at the pool about every problem she was having at home. Because of that, many people knew everything about her, and the shit hole her kids lived in. Why blame me? Many people could have called Social Services, and as it turned out, many had. I didn't want to get Nana Anna in further trouble with Uranus, but at this juncture, I felt that it was still wise to keep her guessing. It was not that I was afraid of her. The hell I say. I had no idea what this crazy woman could or would do, like pouring sugar into my gas tank, or hiring a hit man. We were all concerned about her temperament because of her mental state.

One-way conversation over, I returned to my apartment to clean up the mess I had made.

Well fans, you guessed it. Uranus got her car out of hock for the time being. She needed transportation and no one would haul her around this time. To make matters worse for her, the car failed to get her around safely. Go figure. It wasn't working before, so why would it work now? The car was a pile of junk to begin with; it ran terribly, had no brakes, and needed work on the transmission. The car had so many problems that she was forced to park it somewhere and rent an expensive sports car for the short time she planned to remain home in the USA.

It had now become totally evident to us that Uranus had no intention of ever letting Nana Anna use the car, or fix it for that matter. She spent the money the get the car tags for nothing. Then she rented an expensive sports car. The big question to us was, where had she come up with the money? She had said openly that she was totally broke. Was she mattress dancing somewhere?

I now had become an untouchable to her, a traitor, and a horrid monster beast that had lied to her about registering Tommie, and disrupted her precious plans for her little trip to Viet Nam. I forced her to come home to her damn kids for no good reason at all, and much worse, back to Nana Anna and the stool pit they lived in. Had she forgotten that the kids had been taken and were in Foster care?

She harped endlessly at Nana Anna, saying that she was totally pissed off about Viet Nam, and the fact that the passports for her kids had not come back yet, so they couldn't go with her on the trip as she had planned. My goodness, she would not even get the chance to catch the bird flu, so she could send it home with Grope as a memento gift, along with more poisonous bugs and snakes from the area. It was all just so damn unfair – NOT!

Uranus announced to Nana Ana that she was going back to Iraq as soon as Moe came to take over the children and she could then boot her out on the street. Yeah! Moe was back in the picture for the time being. She would go back to Iraq for at least another year, maybe longer. She liked it there and was having fun while making big bucks. Honestly, Uranus was playing cards she didn't have, and there were not many options left for her. She wanted out badly, and soon. She figured she could pull it off. At least that is what she thought. But she was not thinking right.

CHAPTER 36
CHOICES, CHOICES, SO FEW CHOICES

All was not going as planned by Uranus. You see the kids, Tommie and Grope, defied Uranus' commands, entered the pool area before her and rushed directly to us to visit and play. Uranus, on the other hand, followed the kids into the pool area and lowered her skinny, pasty body, clad in a skimpy teeny-bopper bikini, at the other side of the pool. She immediately gave us a nasty look, then faced away from us, and started making phone calls on her cell phone. She seemed furious that the kids defied her orders and came over to visit with us. However angry, she remained calm and composed, not wanting to make a scene at the pool in front to so many people.

She called the kids over to break some news to them about Moe. "Moe isn't coming," Uranus whined to her daughter at the pool. This information was quickly relayed back to us, lounging on the other side of the pool deck. Disappointment creased Uranus' already stressed out face. Nana Anna was no longer and option, Moe was out, and her escape options were running out. Curly, the father of the kids had already called her, offering to take the kids for as long as she was in Iraq. Uranus laughed into the phone and said a flat NO! Her hatred of him was just too deep. She had hung up on him. This nasty act was a big mistake.

Time was flying by, and Uranus was seeing her plans of returning to Iraq for another year vanishing before her beady red eyes. Booby couldn't take the kids either, well – maybe

Grope for a while. But Booby is unemployed and has a husband and two active kids and pets in a tiny, two bedroom apartment. Booby has a big heart, but little means and a crowded environment for the kids, especially with Grope and his nasty fetishes. But you already know this. Uranus knew the courts would flatly reject any ideas she had. So Uranus sought out another friend up north to watch the kids. The woman, a forty year old single parent, pregnant with young kids at home, was not a good candidate. The courts would not approve of her either. Then she called a distant relative in New Mexico.

Later, when she heard of this, Tommie flatly refused New Mexico to her lawyer (yes Tommie had a lawyer), because Tommie wanted to stay in her current school. Actually, she wanted to live with Cherry.

Uranus' steel trap mind finally went into melt-down. She understood that she must quit her job and return home. My goodness, what a revelation! She knew this act was the only way to keep possession of the kids and retain child support. She had already received a job offer locally, but no where near as lucrative as the one she currently had in Iraq. Would she get the job? Did she really want it? That was yet to be determined. Her choices had virtually evaporated; she also knew that she must find a way to return to Iraq so she could resign from KBR and get another two weeks pay, plus catch a free flight home. That way, she could also ship the treasures remaining in her hooch back to the US. The alternative of not returning to Iraq was unimaginable. She would lose her treasures and owe KBR a lot of money. Yes, that is where the phantom money had come from, a big advance in pay, premised on her return to work.

CHAPTER 37
SELMA PROMISES THE MOON BUT DELIVERS CAULIFLOWER

Ms. Selma, the CPS Social Worker assigned to Grope and Tommie's case called each of us and listened attentively to what we had to say. She took notes over the phone, and promised to get back to us. Ms. Selma was young and seemed to be a caring person. We learned later that she was the individual crying when she left the courtroom after Guido had his day, the CPS lawyer failed to do anything, and the Judge sat there in his chair, hanging on to every word Guido said, ignoring the CPS lawyer.

It didn't take us long, however, to realize Ms. Selma's busy schedule did not allow us much of her time and support. Returned calls were non existent over a long period of time. We were getting frantic. We needed answers. I regularly called for the support group, left voice mails and complained. I eventually became so irate that I called the District Attorney's office to find the Social Services Chief Attorney's phone number. Successful in finding the number, I placed a call to the Chief Attorney; she answered and I complained bitterly. Ms Selma called me back within the hour, apologetic. The squeaky wheel method often works. I figured right that lighting a little fire under her derrière would yield some results. I know that this step was not entirely fair. She, like all the other Social Workers, was overloaded with cases; but we were in a bad position, knowing a court hearing would be held soon and we remained in the dark and totally unprepared to testify. Selma kindly agreed to hold a meeting with us at noon the next day at Katie's apartment. Katie, Cherry and I would attend.

The meeting time with Ms. Selma had come. Katie, Cherry, and I were waiting for her at Katie's apartment. We heard a knock on the door – enter Selma complete with cell phone and notebook. The meeting began. I had several questions listed and most of them she could not or was not allowed to answer. However, she again took notes, because this was the first time we all were together face to face. There was an aura of honesty about her that I liked right off. Selma was one of the caring ones.

We learned from her that another Social Worker would be assigned to the case, and that Selma would still be involved, but only on the legal side of the hearing, and she would not participate with the actual home visits. What home visits, we all thought? There had been no visits since the kids were returned home. Selma informed us that CPS communication with us is restricted by law, but she tried to encourage all of us to hang in there. We were beginning to see some futility in our efforts. She could feel it, and we didn't try to hide it. She told us that winning this case was going to be an uphill battle, because there was no physical evidence of actual abuse, only neglect. Abuse is easy to convict with proof; neglect is not. In fact, neglect prosecution is rarely successful. Was this true? Were we doing all this for nothing? Regardless, we had to try.

The topic of emails came up. Selma offered to turn them over to the attorney handling the hearing. She mentioned again that subpoenas were forthcoming. She assured us that the documents had been generated, but not yet delivered. Yes! We had been asked for evidence. We were promised subpoenas; and they were yet to be delivered by the court. This worried us a bit. Katie and I had prepared our email for her. The hundreds of pages of Uranus' psycho babble backed everything we had told Social Services – everything! We were encouraged, yet apprehensive at the same time. Should we hand over the emails now, wait for the subpoenas, or defy the request altogether? Properly used, these documents would nail Uranus to the wall by illustrating her continuous series of lies in her own writing, but then all would be revealed. Would Social Service hold the information confidential? This was critical. Of course, disclosure would require Guido to be given copies at some point, hopefully later. The proverbial cat would be let out of the bag. Well, he knew anyway, or so Uranus had said.

So far, CPS had been fairly ineffective in handling Guido and his slimy criminal law tactics. We felt that the emails would strike a major blow for the prosecution. Katie and I looked at each other, agreed, and handed two large manila folders over, each crammed with emails. Selma skimmed the documents briefly with widened eyes. "These documents are severely damaging to Uranus and her defense, she said.

However, Social Services' mishandling these documents caused a lot of problems as you will see. Having never been involved with the Child Protective organization before, we were naïve. The incompetence of the Social Services Legal organization went far beyond our comprehension. They had no idea what to do with the emails, or the laws associated with presenting email to the court. Guido took full advantage of that. But that comes later.

Unfortunately, within two days, the email documents and all of the notes taken by Social Services over the phone, notes from the interview when Katie and I first visited the Crisis Center facility, and the notes taken by Ms. Selma at Katie's home, were turned over to Guido. Our names were blacked out, but the source was obvious. That is, all names were blacked out except Cherry's. You see, Cherry had also entertained a conversation with CPS over the phone and her name was scribbled everywhere. Still, no subpoenas had been delivered to anyone. We all felt like we had been hung out to dry.

Of course, sleazebag Guido handed all of the documents over to Uranus right away. This was legal, but considered unethical by the courts. The monster Uranus went ballistic, into an absolute rage, and flew over to Cherry's house to show her what she had just received from her hero Guido.

Cherry was very disturbed, to say the least. The fact that the documents had been released with her name on them was beyond her comprehension, and ours for that matter, and this sounds like a broken record, but no subpoenas had been delivered yet. Selma and CPS Legal had screwed up royally, and Selma knew it.

When showing the email to Cherry, Uranus told her that it showed that Cherry at least had the guts not to hide her name from her, and that she was not mad at her at all (she obviously had other plans for Cherry). Uranus, oblivious to the law, called Katie and me cowards. Then Uranus had the mordacity to tell Cherry that I had intentionally altered my emails to make her look bad, and that Guido would prove it in court. This statement was pure crap. Cherry choked off a laugh and the urge to tell Uranus to go play with herself. Why? She had read the emails we handed in and knew the truth. Good for Cherry. She had guts and a sharp mind. I wish Cherry had punched Uranus in her huge beak, but Cherry is too kind of a person to do that sort of thing.

CHAPTER 38
HERE COMES THE JUDGE

The next hearing was scheduled for the following Tuesday. A second follow-up hearing, should an agreement not be met with CPS, was set for Friday, a little over a week later. We were told by CPS that there was no chance for an agreement. Therefore, the follow-up hearing would be the one at which we would testify. We needed time to prepare and there was just barely enough time to do so. Unknown to us, Guido pulled another fast one, and had the follow-hearing date moved back to Tuesday, a week after the initial hearing. According to Guido, the move was done to accommodate Uranus's plan to return to Iraq the same day as the follow-up hearing, Tuesday. Judge Dread bought it, happy that the follow-up hearing would be held in his court. This breaking news was devastating to us. Katie, the key witness, was scheduled for surgery the same day as the hearing. Plus, Cherry and I had literally no time to prepare. On top of that, School records detailing Grope's Autistic behavior had been subpoenaed, but the schools had not yet responded, and could not possibly make the Tuesday date. We'd been screwed without a kiss; we were up the creek without a paddle. An outright miracle was needed.

Well miracles do happen all the time, or so they say. Ours was about to take place. We had a newly assigned contract CPS lawyer, a bright and experienced woman named Paris Mason.

Best of all, she was quite familiar with Guido and his slimy borderline illegal tactics. She was armed to the teeth and ready to devour him for lunch. The miracle had more to offer. The scheduled Tuesday hearing was postponed to Thursday, because Guido couldn't make it for some reason. He made the nasty comment at the time of his postponement request that a hearing wasn't necessary to begin with, because the only real issue to deal with had to do with a sick dog. Was he calling Uranus a sick dog? Well, sick bitch is a pretty fair description of Uranus.

To our immense pleasure, the rescheduled Thursday hearing began on time, and with a new Judge, one who had prepared. The hearing lasted about two hours, during which Guido was literally crucified by both Paris Mason and the presiding Judge. The Judge reprimanded Guido in front of everyone, and Guido fell back in his chair holding his hands over his face. Ever see the TV ad about embarrassing moments and wishing you were someplace else, like on a desert island somewhere? This event would have made a perfect episode. Guido wished he had never met Uranus, and we were glad that he had. Guido's dirty drawers were exposed. The door to nail Uranus had been opened again.

First of all, and thanks to the competent Judge, we were granted a postponement of the hearing we were to testify at. The delay was set for over a month, after Uranus' return from Iraq. The delay gave our team plenty of time to prepare our testimony. Even better, our star witness Katie would be recovered from surgery, and raring to go. Guido had agreed to the postponement at first, and then proceeded to strongly object, realizing the huge advantage he had just handed us. Ooops! This move gave the Judge another opportunity to embarrass Guido in front of everyone, and she did with a big smile on her face. He flopped back into his chair again, hands covering his purple face. Furthermore, Uranus had offered NO

PLAN as ordered, and no one had been approved to watch her kids while in Iraq. No agreement could be made. Another hearing was ordered by the Judge for the following Tuesday, at which Uranus must present her detailed plan, otherwise the court would decide what action to take while Uranus was in Iraq. Events were definitely moving in a good direction.

CHAPTER 39
D-DAY APPROACHES

U ranus had arranged to depart on her final trip to Iraq the following Tuesday, after her court hearing. She still had no plan, but she had a skimpy idea for a plan, and it involved Cherry and Booby. Yes, Booby was a shoe-in, and she would work on Cherry big time. Uranus figured that the court would allow Booby to watch Grope for at least a month and Cherry would be a no-brainer.

She would convince Cherry to watch Tommie. No problem! Cherry loves Tommie.

Knock, knock! "Who's there?"

"It's Tommie; Can I come in and play with the dogs?"

"Of course you can," replied Cherry.

"However, isn't it a little late at night for you to be out?" It was after nine in the evening.

Cherry opened the door and there stood Tommie, with mommy dearest standing outside the visual range of the peep hole in the door.

"Do you mind if we talk for a bit while Tommie plays with the dogs?" asked Uranus, with a cheesy serpent-like grin.

Cherry, not too pleased with the deception, reluctantly invited them both in. Martin, Cherry's husband, while sitting in front of the TV in the living room, just shook his head in disbelief, but remained silent. Martin would not even look at Uranus and acknowledge that she was there, knowing fully what she was, and this avoidance bothered Uranus a lot. After all, she was the hottest woman around, in her mind at least. The manner in which Uranus looked at him, Martin imagined that Uranus must have been thinking:" How 'bout a threesome while Tommie plays with the doggies?" NO THANK YOU VERY MUCH. ICK!

For the next hour, Uranus babbled lie after lie, but Cherry saw right through them. As mentioned earlier, Cherry had read the emails that Uranus herself had written, and clearly saw the spin on what she was saying. As usual, Uranus repeated herself over and over, pointing out all the compelling reasons why Cherry should take Tommie while she was gone. "I will talk to Tommie every day on the phone to make sure she behaves."

Finally, to get rid of her, Cherry said that she would think about it. The timing was good because Cherry's husband had heard enough and was about to step on Uranus like a legless cockroach! CRUNCH!

The nightly visits with Cherry continued for another couple of days, plus daily and evening phone calls, even to Cherry's work. Uranus was relentless. Cherry kept putting her off, claiming that she would need to talk to her husband about it, and he was currently busy. Monday, the night before the final hearing, Cherry called Uranus and told her that her husband had said NO! His word was final. This was a major blow to Uranus. She had no plan, no options. Her goose was cooked. Or was it? What will the court decide? Was it Foster care for the kids?

CHAPTER 40
HERE COMES THE JUDGE

It was Tuesday, the 6th of the August, and Uranus was packed and ready to depart for Iraq. The court hearing started in the early morning to allow her to reach the airport in time for her overseas flight. The court learned at the hearing that Uranus had no plan. She babbled excuses but her solution was pure vapor; leaving both kids at Booby's for a month. However, Child Protective Services did have a plan, and much to Uranus' chagrin; the plan was agreed upon and accepted by the court. The court ordered Uranus to return home from Iraq within two weeks, not a month as she had planned. If she failed to return on time, she would lose the children permanently. Curly, the children's father, had been asked by the court to fly across the US to stay with the children until the 19th of the month, and he agreed. Until he arrived, Cherry had accepted the court's request for her to watch Tommie. Yes, she had agreed to the court appointment, but not Uranus' request. This pissed Uranus off immensely, and she immediately added Cherry to her special shit list. Furthermore, Booby's home was rejected for long term care, but she was allowed to watch Grope for three days only; until Curly arrived. This was a good thing.

SLAM DUNK for the good guys, and a gavel up the butt for Uranus. Uranus was raging mad as she stormed out of the courtroom, tears in her eyes and unraveled flaming hair flying behind her ugly head.

CHAPTER 41
IMMEDIATE DEFIANCE

Uranus was still in the courthouse somewhere, or off getting a quickie from Navy boy one last time before departing for Iraq when Dumpy was taken by BRAT (Basenji Rescue and Transport). BRAT told us later that Uranus had finally admitted physical abuse of the dog to them. Exactly what abuse she admitted, we did not learn just then. However, we found out later from a friend at BRAT that Grope had shoved a dime deep into the poor dog's vagina just for kicks, a sick and morbid experiment. Worst of all was that Uranus knew that he had done this all along, letting the dog suffer, and hiding the truth from everyone, including BRAT. She had taken the dog to another Vet to insure secrecy. We were hoping the courts would hear of this admission of guilt at some point. But they didn't.

The sad part about the removal of the dog from the apartment was that Tommie was home alone with Grope when BRAT came to the door, and she had to give up the dog herself, with no one to comfort her. Giving up Dumpy broke her poor little heart, and it broke ours as well. But it was best for Dumpy. We were sure that Uranus would replace the dog with a camel spider, a python, a rat, or something creepy.

Uranus arrived home, packed up the last of her stuff and was ready to depart for Iraq. Her rental car was jammed full with her personal bags and Grope's Bionnacle collection. Katie and I sat at the corner café watching her load up to go. It was such a pleasure to see her leave. However, we were soon surprised to see both Tommie and Grope being squeezed into the car. We immediately realized that Uranus had no intention of taking Tommie to Cherry's, who lived in the same complex, within walking distance just across from the pool. There was no way to drive there. We assumed correctly; she was taking both children to Booby's, in absolute defiance of the court order. Big shocker, huh!

Katie quickly placed a cell phone call to Cherry and informed her exactly what was going on. Cherry called Uranus immediately and demanded that she drop Tommie at her home or suffer the court's wrath. We could see Uranus arguing and pleading with Cherry, but she reluctantly caved in when Cherry gave her the final ultimatum, Tommie was to go to her house now, or police and jail for Uranus. We were all hoping for the latter.

It was then that Uranus spotted us watching her from the corner café and she immediately realized what we had done. Uranus was blistering hot. We could see steam blowing out of her ears and nose. We waved goodbye to her with gritty eat shit and die smiles on our faces. The bitch yanked Tommie's bags out of her car, threw them on the ground, screamed obscenities into the air, and sent Tommie, bags in hand, to Cherry's apartment alone. So much for motherly love!

Uranus jumped back into the rental car, slammed the door hard and peeled rubber down the street – leaving almost a city block of rubber and smoke rising in the air. Uranus was obviously in a flaming rage. We muttered "Eat dog dirt and die BITCH." Go play with RPG's. Step on an IED! Get AIDS and die you spiteful snake! Nasty words were not nice, but they did make us feel better. We had squashed her defiant plans, and we really felt good about it.

Cherry called Social Services and reported to them what Uranus had just attempted to do. They said that her actions would be duly noted, as if that would do any good.

Well, at least the Psycho was gone again, for a while anyway.

CHAPTER 42
QUIET ANTICIPATION

For three days there was total peace, even a fun birthday party at Katie's that Tommie and Cherry both attended. We were all able to visit with Tommie. We had missed her. It was difficult at first because she had been programmed rather successfully by Uranus.

But Tommie did begin to warm up to us. You see, Uranus had demanded that Cherry not let either Tommie or Grope see or speak with any of us while she was away. We were evil, but she told Cherry that she was a good person. Oh my, what a quick change of attitude. Cherry, in turn, coldly told Uranus that she could go pound sand, and that Uranus was no longer in control. Cherry would decide just who Tommie could visit with. Uranus must have screwed every male at Camp Fallujah that week to relieve her rage, because she screamed obscenities again as she hung up the phone. Perhaps she took care of her rage herself, with a rubber coated broomstick, or possibly with her roommate - whatever!

Uranus was out of our hair and the stress we all felt turned into a blissful peace, with hopes the children would adapt quickly with their father and that Uranus would get stuck in Iraq for – forever!

CHAPTER 43
THE GATHERING

Curly arrived late Friday evening. We were waiting for him at the local 5 Guys outdoor restaurant across the street from our apartment complex. Our intent was to make him feel welcome and comfortable while meeting Tommie. Although ordered by the court to remain with Curly, Grope would stay with Booby for the night and come home tomorrow. This seemed like a logical thing to do. Having both children dropped on him at once would be overwhelming. While we sat outside wolfing down hot dogs, peanuts, and fries, Tommie took a walk with Katie's husband Jack and daughter Melissa to Burger King, just down the block. This would give us some time with Curly when he arrived.

Curly parked his rental car and was directed by cell phone to where we were sitting. We met and chatted for a short time. It became evident to all of us that he was genuinely concerned about the children and cared for them deeply. We had suspected as much, despite Uranus' blubbering about how he disliked and avoided the kids at all costs. In truth, he had avoided Uranus, and who wouldn't.

Our eyes were filled with tears when Tommie finally met her father a few minutes later. She had the biggest smile we had seen on her face for a long, long time. Both father and daughter held onto each other, not wanting to let go. All of the filthy lies Uranus had told Tommie about her father vaporized the second they met. The moment was golden and surreal. I imagined that tremors ran through Uranus's sick mind when this event happened – or was that a self induced brain fart.

As a group, we chatted for the entire evening and were finally run off by the Café workers as they were shutting down and cleaning up. The entire evening was magical. We understood that Curly had been fully saturated with knowledge about Uranus and the horrors she had been up to. We hoped he believed us and stated that we had written email from Uranus that backed us up. The information was overwhelming, and entirely truthful. Yes, perhaps our prayers for the children would soon be answered.

The balloon of happiness burst because the very next morning we learned that Uranus was already on her way home. She was losing control over her kids and she knew it. She had spoken harshly to Booby and Curly, issuing orders to never allow contact with me or Katie "or else." She was justified in her suspicions that Curly was disobeying her demands and allowing Tommie and Grope to see us. She had also demanded that Grope be left at Booby's until she got home, but that wouldn't happen. Curly flatly refused. The bitch became a raging lunatic over the phone.

We found out later why Curly had issues with watching Grope. Someone had told Curly that Grope was molesting Tommie on a regular basis, and they had to be separated. Because of this, Curly was deeply concerned of the possibility, and preferred that Grope sleep at Booby's. Three guesses who told that to Curly. We only needed one guess. What a scheming bitch! She was playing all her cards and saying whatever it took to ensure the court orders would be violated, and she would do or say anything to get her way. The scary part was this: was Grope molesting Tommie? Did Uranus know this, and do nothing about it?

We were all joking that Uranus' helicopter might crash and burn on the way to Baghdad, or she would fall out of it from 4,000 feet and feed the scorpions. Unfortunately, that didn't happen. At least we had a few more days before Uranus would arrive back.

Monday night, Curly's partner Brady flew into town. We met him at another gathering on Tuesday night. Katie and family, Cherry, Nana Anna, and I all gathered at the same outdoor café where we had originally met and waited. We were looking forward to meeting Brady. We had been told by Uranus that Brady did not support Curly and wanted nothing to do with the children. This, of course, was another fabrication from Uranus's sick and festering mind. The evening was another success and the kids were all as happy as could be. Grope was in his element, and playing with all of us, placing his hands on our heads and sucking out our brains, and hunting for bugs to eat. We all felt like a close family would feel on a holiday gathering. The evening was, again, magical. The thought still remained in the back of our minds that the bitch from hell would be home soon, but we temporarily tried to put that aside, at least for the evening. What would happen next? We had to plan.

CHAPTER 44
POSSIBILITIES

Foremost on our minds was the wish that Curly could gain custody of his children and leave the State before Uranus arrived home. We found out that neither Uranus nor Curly had legal custody. Unfortunately, time was too short for Curly to obtain custody and leave. However, some ideas came to mind that opened a few doors.

Uranus had sent email to Curly stating that she was broke, jobless, and needed money. Don't ask how we knew of this, but we did have a great "friends" network. Uranus was overdrawn again at the bank, had used all of the child support money, and was on the verge of being charged with fraudulent check-writing. How could this help us in our cause? Nana Anna was the answer.

We needed to somehow convince Nana Anna to leave the apartment. This would require some preliminary work on our part. I went to Tom, the Maintenance Manager of the Apartment building, who disliked Uranus immensely and asked him if he would like to help us get rid of Uranus for good. The plan would be simple. She was broke and jobless. We knew through the network that Uranus had attempted to remove Nana Anna from the lease so she could kick her out on the street. We also knew the request was answered with a written denial. Uranus had no credit and could not qualify. Without Nana Anna, Uranus would be evicted. Yes, this could be her undoing and open the door for

Curly to gain custody of the children. The Maintenance Manager thought this plan was a good idea and agreed to talk to the Apartment Complex Manager and ask her to release Nana Anna from the lease, on the grounds of physical and mental abuse from Uranus. There was a compelling need. There was also a letter from a doctor backing this up. There was a chance.

Secondly, Katie talked to Nana Anna, and convinced her to get out of the apartment as soon as possible. We were all afraid for her. Nana Anna agreed to talk to the Apartment Manager to see if she could be taken off the lease without penalty. If this was granted all that was left to do would be to find her a place to live.

It just so happened that we are friends with one of the managers at the local Café – our gathering place. She joined us one evening and said that there was a chance that a room would open up with her in her townhouse nearby. If all of the pieces fell together and Uranus was evicted, had no job, no money, no checking account, and no phone, Curly could ask the court for custody and it would most likely be granted immediately.

Curly and Brady already owned a three bedroom home with a big pond for Grope to catch pollywogs and bugs. There were also several great schools nearby. Most importantly, both Curly and Brady wanted the kids badly. They had good jobs, were solid financially, and would easily pass any inspection given them. Could it be?

Yes, there were a lot of pieces of the puzzle that needed to fit together, but with a lot of prayer, and a little luck, this could be pulled off without a hearing, and the kids could be with Curly by the end of the month.

And what would be best for Uranus? She could return to Iraq and stay there forever - eat sand and grow old! Maybe get swallowed by a huge sandworm. Ooops! Those only exist on Dune. Well, maybe we could beam her there.

CHAPTER 45
DELAYS CAUSE
DEPRESSION TO SET IN

A song by Paul Simon kept ringing in my head; at least the tune was there. The title and lyrics, however, had evolved to "Fifty Ways to Kill a Monster." The monster was in my dreams every night – and the monster was skinny and pasty white ugly, with squinty blue eyes, red stringy hair; her beak of a nose had become huge because of her pathetic lies, and her tongue was long, greasy, black, and forked like a snake's. She wore skin-tight Tinkerbell teeny-bopper jammies, and walked the night upright without shoes.

Uranus would be home in a day or two, maybe even tomorrow, and we had spent a lot of time working with Nana Anna, trying to convince her it would be best for her to leave the apartment. Taking our advice would solve a multitude of problems for her and cause just as many for Uranus. Nana Anna did talk to the Apartment Management Office but the wrong person, and the lady did not cooperate and offer her any relief on breaking the two year lease. This hurt us a lot. She would try again with our help.

Uranus had called Curly every single day, sometimes more often, ranting and raving about how horrid Katie and I were and that he absolutely must not see or talk to us. She just would not let that go. We were out to get her. We were monsters. We were evil liars. Curly told us that he asked Uranus "why do you say all this?" and she replied "because they are going to testify against me in court." Of course she didn't know that our email was now in his hands and that he had read at least the highlighted parts. There were several nasty and false statements she wrote about Curly and Brady that they both found particularly interesting.

Well, at least she got the part about us testifying against her right. She also complained bitterly to Curly that he had not yet called her beloved lawyer Guido and talked to him. We all assumed that Uranus was still under the impression that Curly would defend her in court. She must have felt that she had him under control. Maybe that impression was a good thing for her to think for now. When Uranus arrived home again, everything would turn sour - putrefy. We prayed that Curly could stand up to her evil serpentine tongue, hold his temper and not throw her off the balcony - in front of the kids anyway. Sadly our hatred of her was growing daily; we could not handle her madness.

Katie and I were both getting sick to our stomachs, unable to sleep, and literally stressed to the max about the whole custody fiasco. CPS' lawyer, Paris Mason, was trying to be honest with us and told us that it would be virtually impossible for us to win in court. She was going far beyond the call of duty and perhaps legal ethics in keeping us informed, at least explaining family law policies. Bottom line, Curly needed to get a lawyer and file for custody in Circuit Court, a system completely separate from Children's court. There would be a long process, and an expensive one, but he could win out in the long run. We were running out of time.

I asked Paris Mason: "Why go to court at all if we we're going to lose?" Her answer was simply that we must try. I mentioned to her that CPS had no idea what we were going through, the pain and anxiety we encountered daily. We desperately needed some form of encouragement from them. Selma was a non-entity to us and unreachable, but a friend.

Depression was setting in for all of us. Humor of any kind was hard to find. We joked about Uranus stepping on a land mine in Iraq over and over, silently wishing that it would happen. When the news came out about multiple bombings in Baghdad, as sad and terrible as that was, we joked that perhaps she was a victim or the psychotic bomber – no such luck. Maybe her plane would crash on the way home – and hopefully she would be the only casualty. Maybe she would fall down the stairs and break her skinny neck. A fatal case of the bird flu was also a nice thought. All of these were quite grim thoughts and morally wrong, but we feared the worst and had to break the tension somehow. The stress was just becoming too much.

Then the idea came up about throwing an ongoing party in her apartment when Uranus arrived home from Iraq. She would see the apartment loaded with all the fast foods that she claimed were poison. We laughed thinking of Grope and his face smeared with pizza and Taco Bell "YUMMY FOOD", with scraps of cardboard and paper all over her "clean" floor. What would the look on her face be like if she walked into that?

She would scream "GET THE HELL OUT OF MY HOUSE."

We would all reply in unison "NO, Nana Anna invited us. Join in with us or leave or perhaps we would say that we intend to do this every evening until the kids are taken away from you." Yeah! Dream on!

CHAPTER 46
CONCERTS AND ALMOST FISTICUFFS

U ranus arrived home in record time. How she did it is still a question. Somehow she had borrowed more money and caught an early flight. Her arrival was quiet. Brady had moved into a hotel to reduce any negative issues from Uranus. The evening after Uranus' return, Curly and Brady were scheduled to take the children to a movie. Uranus announced that Tommie was to appear in a concert at school and could not go to the movies. She asked Curly to go to the school concert together.

Tommie participated in the concert by playing beginning saxophone. The evening was charming until Uranus, Curly, and Tommie exited from the auditorium. There Uranus spotted Katie and her son walking toward their car. Uranus stormed over to Katie and shouted for all to hear "How dare you. How could you ruin my daughters evening by showing up here? You have ruined everything."

Katie turned around, stood her ground, and faced Uranus nose to nose. "Listen, Bitch. Tommie invited my son. They are friends at school, and he wanted to see her perform. Unlike you, I don't let my children run about at night without supervision. I came with him. So you shut your filthy mouth or I will shut it for you, right here, right now." Uranus turned away and stormed off muttering to herself.

There is one thing in this world you must understand. Katie is not a person to reckon with. She could have squished that former Marine slut like a June bug hit by a sledge hammer. You don't mess with Katie and get away with it. You go girl.

CHAPTER 47
THE WITCH OFFERS IT UP

Uranus and Curly spent his last weekend in New Jersey on the road visiting her friends, Booby and whomever. The kids went along on the trip and that made Curly happy. Today would be his last full day together with the children until he returned for the upcoming hearing. On the journey Curly endured the endless psycho babble spilling from Uranus's skinny mouth. He tried to tune her out and concentrate on the kids, enjoying their company.

The day quickly passed into night. They arrived home and Curly fixed dinner for all of them. Since this was a school night, the kids were sent to bed around 9:30. Uranus was happy to see them go to bed, even though she never set a bedtime for them, and they were usually scampering around the house like mice until late hours.

Changing into her skimpy teeny bopper jammies, Uranus slinked back downstairs to Curly with a toothy come get it grin and said, "You have no place to sleep tonight. Would you like to come upstairs and sleep in my bed with me? It's OK with me Curly; just don't hog all of the covers." Did she know that he had been sleeping in her bed while she was away?

Curly held back bile building up in his throat and gagged as he replied, "I'll take the floor, thank you very much." This was such an obvious ploy by Uranus. Wouldn't Uranus love to announce out loud to the court: "Curly and I are tight again; we have been sleeping together. Isn't that just yummy?" She would also revel in telling Brady the news. Curly held back further comment. Uranus tried to hide the rejection, but it didn't work. She silently thought "Gay or not, no man can refuse me." So she gave him a "your loss" look and wiggled her skinny ass, as she slithered up the stairs to bed - alone.

CHAPTER 48
LET ME OUT OF HERE

U ranus had been sweet as cane sugar to both the kids and Curly, while he was there. She played the perfect mommy. She treated Curly as her best friend in the world, and babbled on endlessly as if they were still a couple. But Curly saw right through her mask. He was packed and, ready to go. As he prepared to leave, Uranus started crying and asking "but what about our relationship?"

Curly gagged a response: "Relationship? There **is** no relationship," he said tersely. He fled out the door, leaving the apartment as quickly as he could. She was making him sick. The second he drove away, Uranus' face grew dark, at least as dark as a pasty, pale face can get. Her face became contorted, pools of evil, and she reentered her darkened, psychopathic rage. Immediately, the kids and Nana Anna became terrified of her, and slinked off to their rooms to keep as far from her as possible.

Curly immediately called Katie and explained why he had bailed out. "Can you believe it?" he said. "She actually asked me to sleep with her. She is totally crazy. She ranted, and raved, and cried, and begged me to back her in court." He continued, "She repeated herself over and over with lie after lie. Then she asked me about our relationship. There is no relationship." He took a deep breath and said, "My God, I had to leave. I had to get out. I had to get out of there before I did something I would regret.

What a psycho! My poor kids; this must be so hard on them."

If he only knew just how hard it was getting. Tommie reverted back to getting herself up for school, getting dressed, fixing her own breakfast (if there was any food), and walking to the bus stop unassisted. No "good morning." No "Have a nice day." No "I love you." No hug! She shuffled along, head down and a deep, sad expression on her face. She was miserable. Grope was not to be seen anywhere.

CHAPTER 49
CURLY CALLS FOR HELP

C urly finally realized the importance of obtaining an in-state lawyer. It was critical if he and Brady wanted the children. So the search began. He had told Katie that he preferred a gay lawyer, or one that was experienced with gay couples and child custody. Having this information relayed to me, I hit the internet and began searching.

Up popped GayLawNet, a large website that contained a list of gay law firms nation-wide. BINGO. From this list, I found one firm that was not only local, but well reputed in child custody cases for gay fathers and couples. I captured the site and forwarded it to Katie. Katie had developed a good friendship with Curly so she would be the primary focal point. I would do work in the background to help all I could. Katie sent this site to Curly so that he could investigate the firm. Their response time to email was a least 48 hours, so Curly needed to focus on this one.

I also found another law firm locally that specialized in the same field. I sent email to this firm and was called first thing in the morning by Sallie Hammer, the chief lawyer in her firm. I was duly impressed with Sallie. I had a great feeling as she explained her abilities and experience. We talked for about an hour, and she agreed to take the case if Curly accepted her. Filled with anticipation, I forwarded this information to Curly via Katie.

CHAPTER 50
CURLY'S OPTIONS

Curly took my advice and called Sallie Hammer first. The discussion didn't last very long. Although he liked her a lot, she required $6,000.00 up front to take on the case. She would not negotiate payments. I tried to explain that lawyers in our State were expensive, and she was cutting him a break. The fee would be less than six months child support. But Curly felt that he could not come up with the money. After all, Uranus had been bleeding him for years with excessive child support (her personal spending account) and if he lost, she was going to go for more. He couldn't take out a loan. His cash flow was too tight as it was.

We all thought: A local hit man might be cheaper. Nah! The idea never came up. Of course Uranus might be thinking the same thing about Katie and me. We wouldn't put it past her.

Curly spent days, calling the entire area looking for a lawyer. He didn't care about the total cost. He was more concerned about making payments instead of cash up front. I guess that says a bit about our legal system. Cash and carry is how it is today. The rich get covered and the poor, even moderate income parents suck hind tit, a term I learned in my youth, while working on a dairy farm.

We all wanted to find a way to help cover the charges, but there was not enough money between us to come up with it. Pro bono work was a dream. Even Uranus was now required to pay her lawyer. She owed him thousands. We all said that she obviously must find a sugar daddy or start mattress dancing for dollars again.

Curly would keep looking. He was getting discouraged. So were we.

CHAPTER 51
PEANUTS, POPCORN
AND CRACKER JACKS

Uranus was crying broke. Did the wicked witch find a job? Time was short with court only days away. Uranus left home most every afternoon, and Tommie mentioned to her friends that they were going to a lot of baseball games. The kids were also late for school because they didn't get home until very late at night. How could she afford to go to the games? Baseball tickets were expensive, although less than Football, Basketball, or Hockey. Uranus had no money – zilch, or so she claimed.

Light bulb again! Was Uranus working for the local AAA Baseball Team? Could it be? Doing what, we wondered? Could she be mattress dancing with patrons under the stands? "Hey ten bucks for a quickie during the inning break." Could she be selling peanuts, popcorn, and cracker jacks to the patrons? Could she be working a ticket booth or selling beer? Regardless, the idea that she was working for the team suggested answers to a lot of questions, but offered up even more. At least she was industrious. I have to give her that. She may be lying on her back for money, but she was not sitting on her derrière doing nothing.

How would this work situation go with the court? Would this job be considered full time? It would be impossible for her to say full time work because she only attended local

136

games, so the job could not be in the office, which requires daily attendance. Uranus was very secretive about the whole thing, and Guido was sure to exaggerate to the court about the level of the job, and the amount of pay she received. Perhaps Guido knew someone in the team organization. He was, after all, a baseball fan. He told me that once. Regardless, Social Services had promised us that they would check her employment to ensure she made enough money to pay for rent, utilities, food, etc. Had she found a sugar daddy? Perhaps! We reserved our doubts whether or not Uranus made enough money. Besides, the season was coming to an end. What then?

Well, tomorrow night the team had a home game. It would be Friday. If she left in the afternoon, we could rest assured that she was working some kind of job at the stadium.

HMMM! We thought. Should we call the stadium and tell them that they have hired a registered child abuser? Nah! Too vindictive! Besides, I had come up with a better idea less apt to be considered as harassment! Besides, she stayed home that night.

CHAPTER 52
A LAST DITCH ATTEMPT BEFORE THE HEARING

I t was after eleven PM and I was in a peaceful sleep.
Knock, Knock; "Who's there?"

"Nana Anna," she croaked. "Can I come in and spend the night on your couch?"

Groan! I put on jeans and answered the door. Nana Anna had only left my apartment a couple of hours ago. In fact, for the last week she spent most of her home time here, sitting on the couch watching TV, until it was time for her to retire. While she stayed in my living room watching home improvement shows on PBS (Public Television) and eating her take out food on a TV tray, I always remained in my bedroom reading, and pounding away on my PC keyboard or writing in my journal.

I felt sorry for Nana Anna, but we had absolutely nothing in common, so I did not chat with her very often while she was in my apartment. She didn't mind being alone with the TV on, and I preferred being alone under the circumstances.

So I opened the door, and Nana Anna came traipsing in with an armload of covers, pillows, clothes, and an alarm clock. "Oh my God," I silently muttered. "She is moving in." ARGGH!

"Uranus and the kids are still up and making a loud racket in the apartment," she said. "I can't sleep and they are intentionally making noise to get to me," she moaned.

I believed her. This is just something Uranus would do. Of course, the kids still had no set bed time. Going to bed was up to them. It was also their responsibility to get up and make it to school on time, but we know all that. Uranus wanted Nana Anna out and NOW! The kids noise helped exacerbate the situation so she encouraged late night activities. Uranus had become profoundly spiteful.

So, spend the night she did. Nana Anna left for work by the time I awoke from a fitful night's sleep. With guests, I never feel comfortable getting up and walking out of my bedroom during the night to use the single bathroom. Each time I put on something to cover up, and that was a nuisance. I just did not feel at ease with non-family staying in my apartment. Her visits got old fast, but what else could I do. I just despised Uranus and her nasty tactics more and more.

Around noon the next day, I called Katie to see what was going on. There was nothing new to report. Cherry had called me shortly thereafter, and sounded dreadfully tired and upset. She was hurt and missed Tommie terribly. Uranus was watching Tommie like a hawk watches its' prey. Tommie had called Cherry the night before all excited to talk to her, but had to hang up quickly to avoid her mother catching her. It was obvious to Cherry that Tommie feared and, in fact, hated her mother. Tommie knew full well what mommy dearest was up to, but was powerless to do anything about it. Cherry was in agony over this.

It was during a second call to Katie that I had an epiphany. Late night Noise! Sleepless in Arrowhead! This might sound like a reach, but we were down to only a few days before the hearing. My idea could solve our problems.

I quickly dressed and walked to the Apartment Building Management Office where I met the number one manager in charge.

I said slowly and carefully: "I would like to file an official complaint to building management about the family on the third floor of my building. The children remain up late at night (after 11PM on a school night) and the mother plays with them, generating loud noises that vibrate throughout the building. In fact, Nana Anna, who lives in the apartment, has been forced to come to my apartment and sleep on my couch because she cannot get to sleep from the loud noise. She must get up for work in the early morning. This keeps me up, and I consider the entire situation a disturbance and a violation of my privacy."

The manager, in a sympathetic tone of voice, said she agreed, and that she would send the apartment a letter. "That won't do," I suggested. "Your last building manager sent Uranus a formal letter some time ago stating that one more formal complaint about noise and she would be evicted. I want her evicted, and I want her evicted NOW! I have had enough of her."

The manager said that she needed to locate the letter and, if true, she would immediately file for an eviction. Done deal! I told this to Nana Anna later that day at the mailbox. This could solve her problems, because she could get out of any penalties on the financial side, and Uranus would be held responsible for the noise. This pleased Nana Anna to no end. At last there was a way out. And then she asked if she could spend the night in my apartment again. OMIGOD I was tired of this, but remained civil and caved in. I certainly did not want anyone to get the wrong idea. This was a small community.

Of course, should the eviction notice be given, the court would immediately be notified, and with luck, before the hearing date. If only the Apartment Manager would follow through quickly! This was a possible win for the good guys.

CHAPTER 53
A LOT OF RAGE, SO LITTLE ACTION

Yes, CPS was up to their old inept ways again. I had been informed that Francis Stein would be replacing Paris Mason as the prosecuting attorney. This is another perfect example of how ineffective the Child Protective System is. Since most of the CPS lawyers are contractors, they come and go like flu season. Paris had handled Guido, actually crucified him. She was armed to the teeth with background and facts. She was ready to win. So why keep her? Let's get someone else with no knowledge of the case - NOT! I was very upset. Francis Stein is a part time CPS lawyer, young, inexperienced, and the mother of a brand new baby, just perfect for the case – NOT! Well, let's give her a chance and not prejudge her. What choice did we have? NONE!

With only a few working days remaining before the hearing, Francis just started to read our emails and prepare her questions for the witnesses. I called her, and we had a very short conversation because she was "too busy studying the case" to talk – as if I knew nothing or was more a hindrance than a help. Francis said that she intended to meet with Selma the very next day and would call me back to arrange a meeting, when and if possible. Of course, Selma was not current either. Only Paris Mason knew the case from head to toe and she was now out of it, currently on another case. Stupid! Stupid! Stupid!

I received a voice mail the next afternoon stating that

Francis Stein would be out of office and only able to meet with me at the courthouse on the morning of the hearing. I felt as if all of us had been raped by a raging bull. I literally blew a fuse. I had been promised a meeting prior to the hearing at which we could go over all of the questions, including those we suspected Guido would ask. We would be able to discuss what would be said and what limitations would be given in terms of our testimony. The promise had been broken, and I was more than livid. My blood pressure shot up 100 points, and I started feeling severe angina in my chest.

I called Francis back and received nothing but voice mail. I let her voice mail have it with both barrels, holding back nothing. I was fuming mad and told her that I had not officially received a subpoena (signed for) and would not be appearing. I said I was sick and tired of continuous incompetence by CPS and that she was personally about to blow the case to hell, and she could shove the whole damn thing up someplace dark and stinky. I was getting dizzy, raging with disappointment and anger. I slammed down the receiver ready to break someone's neck.

A couple of minutes after leaving Francis voice mail, I caught my breath and called CPS' Chief Attorney. She picked up (miraculous – a real first). I bitterly complained about CPS Legal throwing the case into the sewer by placing a new and part time rookie in front of the sleaze bag Guido. I warned them that they were going to get annihilated in court and I, and the rest of us scheduled to testify on their behalf, were done with them unless immediate action was taken.

I told the Chief Attorney, "I will not be patronized. If we do not formally meet and prepare by this weekend, I will not attend the hearing and screw the consequences. I will leave the State and let you fight it out. Katie, Cherry, and I are all ready and willing to bail out of this and let you sink in your own stink." I was rude, but needed to drive my point across. There was no way we were going to walk into the courtroom unprepared and get slammed by Guido, like all the other lawyers had done in the past. The chief Attorney reluctantly agreed with my grievance, and said that she would call right back.

Five minutes later, I received a very apologetic phone call from Francis. She claimed that we had totally disconnected. She did have Friday and Monday open for a meeting, although these were her days off. As a result, she would need to bring her baby to the meeting. Great! Would the baby be sitting at the prosecutor's desk during the hearing? I settled myself down and calmly agreed to Friday at One PM. Katie and I would attend. Because of work, Cherry would try to attend, but might be a little late. Nana Anna couldn't get off of work, so she would be a no show.

Francis had not spoken to Nana Anna yet. I told her that she was in luck because Nana Anna was being physically and mentally terrorized by Uranus and that she was currently hiding from her by camping out on my couch watching TV. I said, "You can talk to her right now." This surprised Francis a lot. Nana Anna had a lot to offer this case, if and only if she could be made mad enough to build up courage to nail Uranus. I heard of her doing it once. Right now, she was as mad as a hornet that just had its nest hit with a broom and squished.

I told Francis that we had evidence and it was very strong. I said, "Guido will try and refute the evidence in court." It was then that I told Francis that Katie and I had exchanged all incoming and outgoing emails to prove that no email had ever been altered. Guido was in for a real spanking on that one. I offered Francis the opportunity for her to declare me as an expert in the field of email, and she said that she would consider it. Yes, Friday would be an interesting meeting. Kate, Cherry and I would be prepared. We hoped that she would be, as well. Regardless of the encouraging discussion, we had our doubts because of past history, none of it very good.

CHAPTER 54
THE MEETING

Yes, the meeting was on, and Katie and I showed up a few minutes early. We had been informed that Cherry would come to the meeting but that she would be a few minutes late, just as we had thought. At the reception desk, we were told that Francis Stein was going to be a little late herself. Keep in mind that Francis was well aware that we had to be back by three to pick up Katie's son from the school bus stop. Time was tight as it was. We were a little miffed. As it turned out though, Attorney Francis Stein was only a few minutes late, and entered the conference room with her baby and paralegal shortly after we sat down.

Introductions and small talk over, I unfolded a sheet of paper that contained a number of talking points that I had prepared earlier in the week. I asked Ms. Stein if we could cover these items to kick off discussions, and she responded by saying that she would answer each item only to the extent that she was allowed by the CPS Regulations and the laws of the County Judicial System. Handing a copy to her, we began to address each item, one item at a time.

The first point I made was, Guido would try to blame Nana Anna for the entire mess. The real truth of the matter was that Uranus was just as bad a housekeeper, if not worse. I went on to describe Uranus' previous apartment, saying that it was a cesspool and that Nana Anna had never lived there. Katie agreed and said that she had been in the house numerous times. It was filthy to the core.

Secondly, I read that Uranus had openly lied to Guido about Grope's wiping his own feces on his walls – or was it Guido that was lying in court when he said it was dog poop? The fact remained that we had email admitting that the poop was Grope's and that he did it all of the time.

Point three was, Uranus was currently putting on a show for CPS, and apparently had at least one of the CPS Social Workers buffaloed. The person was Feather. We had seen them together at the restaurant across the street laughing and carrying on. We pointed out just how good Uranus was at pulling someone into her corner through lies and deceit.

Point four covered the fact that Nana Anna had given her 60 day notice to the Maytag Apartment Manager in writing, which had been denied. Nana Anna had to leave the apartment because of the severe physical and mental abuse being inflicted on her by Uranus. In fact, Nana Anna had a doctor's note stating that she must leave the abusive environment as soon as possible. It was clear that Uranus, being totally self serving, would not agree to leave the apartment and would use any and all means to find the money for rent.

I thought to myself that Uranus' head was so far up her rectum, it was a wonder she could breathe. She was so full of crap that perhaps her head wouldn't fit anymore. I am surprised her eyes hadn't turned brown by now.

Back to reality here: Unfortunately, Francis Stein told us that if she couldn't pay the rent in time, any eviction would come too late to do us any good in court. This was disappointing.

Point five was a request for CPS to actually check into Uranus' finances to ensure she had a job sufficient to pay her rent and support the children in the months to come. They assured me that they would, but Katie and I were not convinced.

CPS had said many things in the past and had not followed through. This was a contract lawyer speaking, not CPS itself. CPS was not even present at the meeting.

Point six stated that Nana Anna had already terminated the home phone. This would force Uranus to at least supply Grope with a cell phone. We did not know that she already had purchased a cell phone for Grope to use.

Point seven stated that Nana Anna intends to close her checking account and retrieve the credit/debit card, removing any banking ability from Uranus. Although the items are all in Nana Anna's name, the accounts contain only Uranus' money. This task will be done before the hearing. Keep in mind that Uranus had been unable to open a checking account before because of her bad credit history, and it has not improved at all. Does Uranus have the credit to open an account now? None of us believe she does; but then again, Uranus does things that seem almost magical – dark side magical.

Point eight stated that we had been told by Curly that Uranus told him she is totally broke – except for her child support money. She had lied in court and claimed that she does have money coming from her former employer. In truth, according to Curly, she does not have another check coming from her employer. Nana Anna is prepared to prove it in court, because all of Uranus's money is in the account Nana Anna opened for her to use (the one to be closed). Nana Anna will provide evidence to the court proving a year of reckless spending and illegal check writing causing the bounced checks due to insufficient funds. Nana Anna is on the verge of being charged for fraudulent check writing because of Uranus' reckless check writing habits. The problem to the court is that that Uranus is forging Nana Anna's name and it might be hard to prove.

Point nine stated that Uranus had been given formal notice

by the Apartment manager's office that any more noise complaints and she would be evicted. I saw the letter, and the office has a copy of it. I said that I had filed a complaint yesterday because Uranus was making huge amounts of noise with the kids very late at night. I said that Nana Anna had banged on my door and woke me after 11 PM and stayed in my apartment on my couch because of the horrible noise they were making. Neighbors under her could validate the noise. They said to me that the noise was bad. I asked them to report it to Management, but feel that they won't. They are not complainers. Regardless, the Apartment Manager said that my complaint may be enough for the eviction, but it would be up to the corporate office to decide. I then told the group that I believe Uranus had put the manager of the apartment under one of her spells. In fact, that turned out to be true.

Point ten announced that Uranus had complained that the emails submitted to CPS were altered by me. I told them Katie and I exchanged many important emails to ensure integrity of data. I also created a CD of all of the emails using Microsoft Image File on Outlook Express mail (which cannot be altered). No email data had ever been altered – unless done by Uranus or Guido. I offered the CDs and my hard drive as evidence to the court if necessary.

Point eleven stated that once, while in my apartment Guido had told me that he knew that Uranus is totally crazy and needs help, but he could not drop her as a client. Of course, that would be my word against his.

And lastly, point twelve stated that Uranus leaves the kids alone at home all the time. We watch and have seen it time and time again. In addition, Nana Anna called one of us each time Uranus left the children alone at home. This neglect has been reported to CPS a multitude of times, but they (Feather) had done nothing about it so far. We felt that the Social Worker

Feather was under Uranus' thumb and this later proved to be a fact.

After going through all of this information Attorney Stein stated, "All in all, the chances for a CPS win in this case are very slim. This is true even though there is strong evidence and Uranus has a long child neglect record. Paramount for a win is for Curly to find a good lawyer and combine the CINA custody case with the hearing."

In other words, everything we have done isn't worth a hill of beans. Bad mothers can get away with everything. Francis Stein admitted off the record that the court was corrupt and biased toward the mother. She also stated that Guido was formidable and would probably win. His chances in Family court would be far less if Curly came through and found a good lawyer.

CHAPTER 55
OUR HERO

That afternoon Attorney Francis Stein became a hero to our cause. She had just given us a statement that indicated we were going to be defeated in court. Then, just before the meeting broke up, she gave us the name of a good Family Lawyer that might take on Curly's case. Leslie Smart was her name. She had worked with Attorney Smart in the past and she said that she would be perfect for the case. She is gay, has a life long-term partner, quite familiar with gay custody issues, a highly experienced Family Lawyer and best of all she owns her own business and would most likely be flexible on cost and payment and meet Curly's terms. Ms. Stein even offered to call Ms. Smart and brief her on the case.

I went home and immediately sent an email to Attorney Smart explaining the details as best I could. I received an email back the very next day stating that she had already spoken with Attorney Stein and was very interested in the case. The one thing remaining to be done was to talk to Curly. I gave her Curly's cell phone number. Unfortunately, Attorney Smart spent the entire weekend playing phone tag with Curly. Fortunately, the voice mail messages got through.

Katie and I picked Curly up Monday afternoon at the airport. Curly brought us up to speed, as we walked to my car in the lot. He was finally able to talk to Attorney Smart, and had made an appointment to see her the following morning. The meeting the following day went exceptionally well, and Curly hired her on the spot. At last we had the break we needed.

The Court had been informed that Curly had a Family Lawyer, and was suing for custody of Tommie and Grope. Attorney Smart would issue the subpoena at court the following morning before the hearing. Score another one for the good guys.

CHAPTER 56
HERE COMES THE JUDGE

Yes, the hearing day had arrived. Katie, Cherry, Nana Anna, and I arrived at court at 8:00 AM, and were anxious to testify. Proceed we did not. Other than going for a cup of coffee, the morning passed with us all sitting in chairs outside the courtroom. We were all nervous as cats stalking a juicy mouse. Lawyers and CPS personnel came and went; Uranus and Guido arrived looking grim and haggard. Uranus had dyed her hair, and it appeared deep red with an orange tint. We all guessed it cost her $400.00 of Curly's child support money. Yep, it had. She was dressed a skin tight black pantsuit, neatly pressed. Her appearance looked professional – right off the street. Nah! She was dressed very nicely; she even looked better dressed than Guido in his dark blue sharkskin suit. However, the look on her face gave her away. Her look was as cold as death.

We had suspected the night before, and were told later that morning, that a continuance had been requested by Curly's new lawyer. We were also informed that Curly's lawyer was asking to combine the CINA (Child in Need of Assistance) case with the custody suit. When this was announced in court, Judge Dread immediately terminated the proceeding, forcing everyone to walk to another courtroom on another floor to see a "Family Court" Judge. We walked along and waited outside the courtroom. Judge Dread would not be part of this process, not

151

yet anyway. Sure enough, the hearing scheduled for today was delayed for another two weeks. Unfortunately, the Circuit Court Judge refused to combine the hearings, and as a result, Curly would be required to return and attend a Family Court hearing in late November, in addition to the CPS hearing in two weeks. Happy Thanksgiving everyone – NOT! We were quite disappointed, but understood the circumstances. The door had been left open for Judge Dread to play coward, and pass all important decisions to the Family Court, possibly causing months of delays and many more trips for Curly.

There was a high point to the day, however. At least we were able to see Uranus receive the subpoena from Family Court, informing her that Curly had filed for full custody of the children. Her pasty, makeup caked face turned dark. She eyed Curly sitting near us and shot him a thin lipped, beady death eyed look of pure betrayal, hatred, and contempt.

Lawyer, $4,000.00; Subpoena, $250.00; Look on Uranus' face, Priceless...

We left the courthouse in great spirits and walked to a popular sandwich place just around the corner for lunch. Minutes later, Uranus and her slimy lawyer walked in. They spotted us, grimaced, turned around, and left. Go eat bugs, we all said quietly.

Now it was back to our homes to remain patient, and await calls from Curly's lawyer the following week.

Curly was scheduled to remain in town until the next day. He tried to arrange to see his children while at court, but Uranus told him that she had other plans and the children would not be available. Curly placed one quick call to his lawyer and squashed Uranus' attempt to block the visit. She had no plans with the kids. She was just being Uranus when she did not get her way - mean, contemptuous, and just plain ugly. She was royally pissed off when told that she had no choice but to let him see the kids.

However, she did manage to limit the visit. Curly could only see them in her apartment after dinner and just before bed. Yeah right. Uranus had never set a bed time for her kids before, but was now imposing rules to upset Curly, to show him she was still in control, and to make mommy dearest look good to the court. As if CPS or the Court ever checked!

Curly departed for home the next morning and had made a number of calls to the children from Katie's house before leaving, but the kids' cell phone was not answered. Later, Uranus called Curly back on Tommie's cell phone and said in a nasty tone: "What do you want?" She was filled with contempt. She informed Curly that from then on she would be listening in on all of their conversations. This initiated another call to his lawyer.

We heard from Nana Anna and Cherry, through their talks with Tommie, that Uranus was brainwashing the kids again and filling their heads with lies that their so-called father was trying to buy their love and that he was a queer, and, as such, very bad person. He really didn't care about them at all. Curly was just a fag putting on a big act. His buying gifts for them and being nice was only because he wanted to get even with mommy, and make her look bad. She even told them that being gay was a mortal sin and evil in the eyes of God. Unfortunately it is in her church, which I left after I heard this directly from the pulpit. I am not gay, but I am sympathetic and disagree with their harassment by others. Over time, the kids swallowed the bait, hook, line, and sinker.

CHAPTER 57
A LITTLE WORK AND MORE DECEIT

The week following the non-hearing, we each received a call from Curly's Lawyer, Leslie Smart. Over the next week, she spent a lot of time with each one of us asking questions but was unable to give us anything in return. Regardless, we were all pleased that she was doing her homework. We were all trying our best to be helpful.

Later the next week, Katie received a call from Curly informing us that his lawyer told him that Uranus was going to plead guilty on all counts of neglect. This news excited us, but we all felt that she was up to something. She had indicated in the call that she wanted to retain custody of the children until the Circuit Court hearing could be held sometime in November. We exploded with that news. The bitch had multiple convictions in multiple States. She had the nerve – the most arrogant audacity, after admitting guilty to all charges of neglect, to request retention of her children. No way. The wicked witch had to go down. The kids had to be taken from her clutches. I felt in my bones that, even though she may admit guilt, she would blame everyone else for the problems, convincing herself into thinking that she was just a victim. I was positive she had something sinister up her sleeve.

This mess had been going on for so long that I began to wonder if I was the one that was mental. I was really guessing at this point, although I am good at that sort of thing, and am often correct. I had prior "feelings" that Uranus wanted to give up the children and eventually go back to Iraq. I knew that she had lied to her overseas employer and in all likelihood would be rehired in her old job if she wanted it, or perhaps given a new opportunity in foreign relations. That field was her dream anyway. But something else was nagging at me, and a phone call from Cherry later that day confirmed my suspicions, and totally rattled my cage.

Only two days from the hearing and calls from Curly were going to Cherry instead of Katie. I had not heard from him once. I understood that I was to pick him up at the airport tomorrow. We were all on pins and needles and my nerves were affecting my blood pressure again. Curly told Cherry that just yesterday his lawyer had told him that Uranus would, indeed, plead guilty to all charges, and because of that, CPS would let her retain custody of the kids, at least until the child custody hearing was completed sometime in late November. This news was quite disheartening. It was like placing a baby in front of a hungry alligator and saying to the predator, "stay put and don't harm the child."

Cherry was told that Uranus didn't even have a lawyer anymore. Guido had bailed out. He wasn't getting paid, and Uranus probably refused to put out to him anymore. Perhaps Guido had not informed CPS of this; that he had resigned. The pro boner bit was still a guess. Regardless, it meant to me that CPS really didn't give a damn about the Children at all. Feather had somehow convinced the lawyers and other Social Workers that it was best to let Uranus have her way for now. We heard that Feather stated to CPS that "Uranus has shown a "new leaf" lately." Little did any of them know the new leaf was pure poison – a scam - a ruse. CPS ought to know statistics show that over 90% of those individuals who have custody of the children at the time of the custody hearing retain custody, especially mothers.

Obviously, Uranus knew that statistic or had found that out somehow.

To make matters worse, there was no question in any of our minds that Uranus planned to obtain passports, legally or illegally, and leave the country with the kids before or just after the custody hearing. Nothing would stop her if she got the papers. With full custody (for the time being) she might be able to sneak the paperwork through the network somehow. I know this sounds paranoid – but I swear Uranus has a Masters Degree in the Black Arts.

Totally frustrated, I told Cherry and Katie that if we lost, I planned to contact the ACLU and try to file a lawsuit against CPS for incompetence. I had a stack of evidence I had gathered over the past several months and felt sure I could at least chop off a few heads. The County Social Services system is badly broken and needs cleaning out. So does the juvenile court system. I was livid and at the end of my rope. I had already prepared a tort of sorts and was ready to nail their chicken-shit butts to the wall. They had disobeyed confidence laws, outright lied to us, and ignored significant evidence. Then they squirreled their way out of the hearing to save face and save money. They never had the kids' best interest at heart. We were being played, used and abused by them.

CHAPTER 58
OUR DAY IN COURT

The CPS hearing day finally arrived. It was 7:30 AM, chilly and raining outside. We all loaded into my Explorer and headed for the courthouse. Would there actually be a hearing? Would Uranus plead guilty? More importantly, would the Court grant her custody of the children? We were all so burned out from stress just waiting for this day. The drive was miserable, with traffic backed up for miles because of the heavy rain. Why Not! It was a gloomy day, and we all dreaded what might happen. The cold and rain did not help our mood.

Pulling away from home, we noticed Tommie getting on the school bus. This was wrong, as the child had been subpoenaed to appear before the Judge. CPS had subpoenaed them and had told us. Uranus was up to her defiant act again. We would wait and see what happened when CPS realized what Uranus had done. This became the primary topic of discussion on the way to the courthouse.

We arrived at the courthouse and entered the building through the security gate. We were in the process of going up to the eighth floor to the waiting area when we spotted Uranus entering the building. She was really decked out this time, dressed to the nines, and looking professional again. There goes another $400 haircut out of Curly's support money and God only knows how much on the new outfit. She didn't have to dress like that. We all knew that she was a pro.

Did she still have a lawyer? Would Guido show up? Damn! Yes to both. Deceit revealed. He needed a haircut, but was dressed in his best blue lawyer garb and had a serious look on his face. He and Uranus sat on the other side of the room waiting for the start of whatever. They were chatting silently and avoided looking at us completely. We did look like a mob, compared to the two of them, especially when three lawyers, a paralegal, and Social Services showed up and joined us. Yes, the white hats had arrived and were charged and ready to roll.

When the courtroom opened a short while later, Uranus and Guido went in first, followed by the CPS gang. We sat in the waiting room but could see quite an animated show going on inside the courtroom. We had positioned our chairs so that we could see into the room through a narrow glass partition in each of the two doors. There was a lot of animation, and we wondered just what the hell was going on. It looked like Guido was screaming mad, and Uranus looked rattled and furious. Guido had his Judge, but apparently the Judge wasn't listening to him. One thing was for sure. Uranus was NOT pleading guilty, as she said she would. Those were planned lies, tactics to catch us off guard, and it did.

After about an hour, the doors opened and everyone came out. The CPS lawyer came over to us and stated that there would be a hearing today. However, the questions we were to be asked were pared down significantly because most of the issues had been agreed upon. This sounded familiar, an old Guido trick. We were told only those items both parties had not agreed upon in court today would be asked. Yep! This was another Guido tactic and it made us very nervous. We were then told that Uranus was chastised by the Judge for not bringing Tommie with her to court. That was what the screaming was all about? So, the hearing would be delayed until Tommie could be picked up at school and brought into the courtroom. Judge Dread would then meet her and chat in private. Twenty minutes later, Tommie showed up with Booby. It turned out that Uranus had thrown a fit and refused to let CPS pick up and bring Tommie to court. We knew Uranus was terrified that Tommie would talk. The Judge, being Guido's buddy, caved in to Uranus' demands. That didn't sit well with anyone, especially CPS. They had planned on talking to her. All of us knew that Tommie had been well "trained" by mom for what she was about to say to the Judge. She had been given a lot of time to brainwash her and Booby would certainly remind her.

At long last, the Judge met with Tommie in the courtroom and the discussion lasted for about fifteen minutes. The hearing began shortly after Tommie left with Booby.

CPS Social Workers were the first on the stand. That took about thirty minutes. Katie followed. She was nervous, but appeared totally confident in the courtroom as we watched her through the glass. The stress on Uranus' face was obvious. We were confident that Katie did a great job. Of course, once she exited the courtroom she couldn't talk about it. Next, Nana Anna was called in and her time on the hot seat lasted less than ten minutes. The CPS Lawyers were very cautions about what they asked her. Then Cherry was called in. Surprisingly, her testimony lasted for quite some time, at least as long as Katie's. She also appeared totally confident on the stand. Cherry was an important witness for the prosecution because of her close relationship with Tommie. Then it was my turn. I was called in after Cherry exited the courtroom. I walked into the room feeling comfortable and quite confident that I could do some damage myself. Before I had a chance to take the seat, CPS asked for a five minute break. After ten minutes, the Judge decided to break for lunch. That was a major letdown for me because I was really pumped and ready to drop a sledge hammer on Uranus.

We ate in silence at a small Mexican fast food place that was not too far around the corner from the courthouse. Actually, the others talked but I had to stay away from them because I had not testified yet. I rushed through lunch because I had to be back and wanted to be ready to go when called.

My testimony went fairly quickly. This was surprising to me. I guessed that a lot of my testimony was accepted already. CPS and Curly's lawyer fired a number of questions at me, and I answered them with ease. Then the question relating to my having altered emails was brought up by Curly's attorney. I had expected to be questioned on that, but not by her. I explained how I had not altered any email and had used Microsoft Photo Image software to capture the original emails sent and received in Outlook Express. I carefully explained that original mail could not be altered and that I did not know how to do it if there was a way.

When finished with CPS and Curly' lawyer, Guido immediately jumped on me with a partial email that I had given the court. I had sent a longer email to Uranus. He showed me Uranus' copy and it definitely had more to it than what I turned in. I responded that I was asked to only turn in relevant material, so I had cut that particular email short. Then I stated to the court that the entire email he was showing me was on the disks I had prepared and given to CPS, including a copy for Guido. Furthermore, I stated that he was asking me about email that was attached to an original message. In other words Uranus had used "Reply" to send her messages back to me. I mentioned to the court that the secondary (piggybacked) messages could be edited and was not sure if it had been edited by Uranus. In truth, Guido's questions should not have been admissible in court. Both the Judge and CPS ignored this. I looked to Attorney Stein for an objection, but none came. Guido knew he had gotten away with it and showed Attorney Stein a copy of the email. She said that she did not have a copy of it; I corrected her and told her that she did have it on the CDs. She looked embarrassed.

Then the shit hit the fan. Guido screamed "What CDs?" Attorney Stein replied that I had turned in two disks to her that contained all my emails, every one sent and received. One copy was, indeed, for Guido but she had not sent it to him and she had not read hers. Guido immediately called for a dismissal, because the CD had not been handed over to him in disclosure. My heart dropped to my stomach. Attorney Stein saved the day by pulling them out of her briefcase, showed them to the Judge, and said that she had not read them because she could not open them on her PC. Thankfully, the Judge bought it. I had clearly told Attorney Stein that she could get the software to read the CDs from the County IT department. I had already checked into it. We could have been screwed right then and there had the Judge wanted to nail us. CPS Legal had dropped the ball – big time. The reason was simple. Like all of the other CPS Attorneys, Ms. Stein had not been given the time to properly prepare her case.

Unfortunately, the Judge being ignorant of email laws, allowed Guido's questions on secondary emails, and I was forced to admit that I had supported Uranus for a long time. I was also forced to say that Uranus was actively looking for a replacement for Nana Anna, but not allowed to describe the ridiculous way she was going about it. Finally my chance came and I dropped a hammer on her head. I stated to the court that I had begged her to come home, several times. I said that I agreed that Nana Anna was overwhelmed. I then said that Uranus should not have gone to Iraq in the first place without someone qualified to watch the children. I had told her so before she left. This hit home. The fact that Uranus knew that Nana Anna was the wrong choice before she left and that Uranus had repeatedly refused to come home when things got bad hurt her case. I made those points very clear to the Judge and he listened to me with interest. Guido kept his mouth shut for once. I repeated that Uranus had written in her emails that she was having too much fun and the kids could just tough it out. These statements enraged her in court. Poison darts flew at me from her eyes. The devil woman had been set on fire.

Attorney Smart proceeded to ask me about my thoughts about Curly and Brady. I stated that for the first time I saw love in the kid's eyes. I heard a parent say I love you to them. I felt that Curly would make an ideal parent and that Uranus was unfit for the task, considering the children as possessions rather than her children and consistently neglecting them. This drew more poison darts from Uranus' evil eyes. I smiled at her in contempt.

I felt drained and unsure whether or not I had made a positive impact. I prayed that I had, and Ms. Stein whispered, "Good job," as I left, but Curly's look at me was passive. That bothered me – a lot.

Once I was dismissed, the hearing continued with Curly. He was on the stand for a long time, maybe an hour. Then Uranus was called to the stand. The impact was immediate and obvious. We could see Uranus on the stand and she was being fried by the prosecution, primarily by Leslie Smart. We later heard from Curly that Uranus was made a total fool of in court. Attorney Smart had repeated my points several times. The Judge was clearly shown that Uranus was a self gratifying, neglectful mother, her financial situation was desperate, she was guilty for leaving the kids alone, she was neglectful in ensuring they were properly taken care of, and she had a long history of neglect to prove it.

The Judge ended the hearing early and scheduled it to be continued the next day. Katie, Cherry, Nana Anna, and I were told by Attorney Stein that it was not necessary for us to reappear.

I offered to take Curly and Brady to court the next morning, but they declined and said that they would prefer to find their own way. We all were exhausted from the long day, and went home and crashed for the night.

CHAPTER 59
THE FIRST FINDING

Sleep did not come at all that night. The morning passed at a snails pace. I was very nervous, as were the rest of us. I had heard from no one, but expected a call when the hearing was over. I had called Katie and found out later that she had, indeed, dropped by the courthouse. Good for her, I thought. I had wanted to do the same thing but decided to stay home as requested. I had a feeling that Curly preferred me not being there. Perhaps he really did feel that I did not do well in court. The long wait for me was agony.

Around 2:30 PM, the phone rang and I jumped to it. It was my son. Rats, I thought. How rude is that. I love my son and his beautiful family dearly, but I was totally preoccupied. During the call, a second call came in. YES! It was Curly. I quickly flipped back and told my son I would call him back and switched back to Curly - thinking thank God for call waiting.

Court was out. The news was not entirely good. Both Uranus and Curly had been placed on the stand twice more today. Social Services had taken the stand as well. Curly told me that his lawyer had again crucified Uranus on the stand and caught her in numerous lies. The Judge did find Uranus GUILTY of blatant child neglect and temporarily removed custody of the children from her. Unfortunately, Judge Dread also found Curly guilty of neglect, claiming that, even though Uranus hid the children from him, he could have found them if he really wanted to. This seemed terribly wrong, but probably true in some way. It became apparent to us that the Judge had no real spine; otherwise he would have taken the children away from Uranus immediately. The issue was that Judge Dread had not done his homework properly, and did not consider or ignored Uranus' past history of child neglect. Even though the kids were now under the control of the court, he allowed the psychotic bitch to keep the children at home until the next hearing. That would be held in November, just prior to the Family Court Custody hearing. Judge Dread was not through. He ordered Uranus to take Tommie and Grope for psychiatric evaluations. Too bad the list didn't include Uranus. She would have failed miserably.

Curly said the Judge had told him to return home and obtain detailed information on special CINA schools, schools with specific programs for children in need of assistance. Furthermore, Curly was to educate himself on Asperger's Syndrome; and to return to court in November; and to file a detailed report for his review prior to the hearing. In the meantime, Social Services in Curly's State would be notified by CPS to perform a background check on him and visit his home. This would be coordinated by CPS in Arrowhead.

Uranus stormed out of the courtroom totally livid and ready to explode. She had expected a total win, and instead she had been handed her head. However, being what she is, her plotting and scheming began to immediately bubble in her sick mind. Losing was not an option and she had some devious planning to do. And evil planning she did, terribly cruel and evil.

CHAPTER 60
THE NOSE GROWS

During the hearing, Uranus had claimed to the court that she had a really good job, and Guido had backed her up. But the truth was that she only had short term work with a temp agency no less, and just before the hearing, she had, in fact, been fired for one reason or another. So in truth, she was flat broke and unemployed to boot. We later learned from Tommie that she was fired because she was "too pretty" and the other women in the office were jealous. One must wonder where that came from. Uranus was probably soliciting clients for a few extra dollars.

As a result of her being fired, and being broke, we all suspected that Uranus would be unable to pay her rent. We were hoping beyond all hope that she would be evicted because eviction would mean that custody of the kids would immediately transfer to Curly. Child Protective Services was not aware of the situation, however.

What ever happened to CPS checking into her employment and income? CPS had dropped the ball again. We felt that the problem was due to Feather. She was now Uranus' buddy, and most likely Feather covered for her, hiding the facts from her boss and the court. Katie and I had discussed the potential situation with the Property Manager and the Manager had said that she would not give an inch to Uranus because she was bad news to begin with. We thought the Manager understood the neglect issue and was on the side of justice.

All of us thought this.

The Property Manager's claim to support us turned out to be total fabrication on her part. In fact, the Property Manager had been totally sucked in by Uranus and she believed all of her lies. The manager now believed that both Katie and I were stalking Uranus unjustifiably. To her, we were determined to crucify Uranus' life and remove her loving kids from her. Uranus was definitely building her set of evil apostles. We also discovered, through one of the children, that Uranus had gone back to the local Church and sought financial help. She had been attending church regularly lately, even though she openly claimed to others that Christianity is too dogmatic, saying that she preferred Islam and other eastern religions to Christianity. The church, like most philanthropic organizations, responded to Uranus and paid her rent for her. They had no idea at the time how much damage they had really caused. But the members of the huge church, over 5,000 members, have big hearts, and willingly gave her the money without question. You see, Uranus had befriended one of the Church Officials, a truly religious woman. I had met her once or twice before and she is truly a caring and loving Christian individual. It was not my place to set her straight. That would be wrong of me, especially since I left the church for reasons I explained earlier.

CHAPTER 61
THE FIRST FINDING

Fall had turned quite chilly. November began with a vengeance. Thanksgiving was just around the corner and the court date was drawing close. Curly and Brady flew into town and moved in with Cherry and her husband for the next two days. Curly had arrived with high expectations. He and his lawyer, Leslie Smart, were loaded for bear and anxiously awaiting for the hearing to begin. Curly had done his homework and filed his reports. Uranus had stated in the previous hearing that Grope's school was the best possible place for him and that there were no schools that could help Grope anywhere near Curly's residence. This, of course, was fabricated bull hockey, and Curly had hard evidence in hand that would squash her twisted facts. Curly lived near one of the best special education schools in the country. Curly had also studied up on Asperger's Syndrome and was totally prepared to answer any question the Judge had to offer. He felt good about his chances. We were all encouraged.

Court opened with high expectations. Curly took the stand and discussed his report that he had already given to Judge Dread. The Judge was exceptionally pleased with Curly's report on local schools. The evidence was overwhelming.

Then the issue of Grope's problems arose. Guido attacked Curly with several questions about Asperger's Syndrome and Curly corrected him on a couple of his questions, stating that what he was asking was not relevant or just plain incorrect. Obviously, Uranus had posed the questions for Guido and did not know what she was talking about. She had entered the courtroom with a pile of books on the subject, but had probably not read them. Before leaving the stand, the Judge told Curly that he was very pleased with his efforts.

Uranus finally took the stand and immediately fell on her beak by telling the Judge that she had not taken her kids in for psychological evaluation. She admitted that she had refused to let CPS assist in this. She presented a number of lame excuses. The Judge was furious at Uranus and scolded Child Protective Services, claiming they were weak and had not performed any part of their job either. Now brought to light was the fact that CPS had not even ordered a background check on Curly, or a check of his home. To make matters worse, Guido finally announced to the court that he was no longer on the case, that Uranus would now be represented by a new lawyer familiar with Family Services. He asked for another hearing delay. This planned move, along with Uranus having defied the Judges demands, forced Judge Dread to once again schedule another hearing. Yep! This fell directly into Uranus' filthy plans. The next hearing would be held after the holidays – in January sometime. This would mean more travel expenses for Curly and more time for Uranus to train the children's minds. The Judge announced that the children would again remain with Uranus. This call was inexcusable, and Curly's lawyer should have immediately objected. Judge Dread also ordered Child Protective Services to oversee the Psychological evaluation of Tommie. He then announced that Grope required no further evaluation, because his condition was already known. To him, Grope was a lost cause and the school issue was resolved. Judge Dread was obviously incompetent. He should have held Uranus in contempt of court; he should have had Uranus arrested and taken the children from her right then. CPS was also incompetent for not doing their job. The real victims here were the kids and Curly. Uranus was getting her evil way. Her plan was now unveiled, to delay the process as long as possible and break Curly emotionally and financially. Uranus would make Curly take leave from work, and pay to travel from home to New Jersey, appearing in court again and again. The "plan" was working. She was going to break him financially and mentally. It was only a matter of time. We all figured out that Guido contributed to the wicked plan, and he had. Break the opponents back by breaking his bankroll.

CHAPTER 62
HAPPY HOLIDAYS

By now, frustration had really set in with all of us. Curly was now home and working hard with his lawyer to prepare for the next hearing in January and saving up money. Uranus was complaining to Feather and the Apartment Manager that Katie and I were stalking her. This, of course was paranoia on her part. I never even saw her. Furthermore, Uranus had to walk by Katie's apartment to reach her garage where she parked her car. Katie could not help but see her on occasion since Uranus' garage was below and adjacent to Katie's fourth floor apartment and visible from her front windows. The Apartment Manager also received an anonymous nasty complaint about late night noise coming from Katie's apartment. Katie received a warning letter from the Management. Katie stormed over to the office and confronted the Manager directly. Katie had been out of town during the time of the complaint and she could prove it. The message had come from Uranus or one of her disciples. She told this to the manager. This did not settle well with the Manager. Regardless of Katie's proof, the manager didn't believe Katie's story about not being home, basically calling her a liar. It was becoming clear that Uranus was winning the psychological battle with her Manager. Uranus was pulling out all of the stops, throwing false stones, being very cunning, and wicked to the core.

Uranus decided to leave the State to visit a supposed relative over Thanksgiving. She loaded her small car with bags of dirty clothes, the Chinchilla, cage and all. She piled in the kids, Tommie in front and Grope in back, sitting him on the dirty clothes, next to the Chinchilla, and his bag of Bionnacle toys. Then she threw Tommie's new pet rat on the dash, told Tommie to sit, and off they went.

Uranus had been instructed by the court not to leave the State, and to inform CPS and the lawyers if she even went out of town, but her defiance of authority was in full gear. This was nothing new. By now we all knew the court and CPS would do nothing about it anyway. Uranus certainly knew. She did tell Curly as she was leaving, that she was going somewhere, but she refused to give him a destination or an address. Curly immediately called his lawyer and she noted Uranus' behavior. CPS was then notified by Curly's lawyer, but Feather took the message, and did nothing with it. Somehow, there was no record of the call ever having been placed. We were concerned whether or not Uranus intended to return. That was paranoia on our part. We should have known better, because she did not take all of her "precious" possessions with her.

Several days after Thanksgiving, Uranus and brood did return - rat and all. The kids had missed a few of days of school, but that didn't matter. They were both failing anyway.

As Christmas approached, the weather turned freezing, and there was ice and snow on the ground. In very the early morning, Katie spotted Tommie going to the bus stop in shorts. She asked Tommie about that and Tommie replied, "My mother doesn't care what I wear and I don't have any clean clothes. I don't have any long pants that fit" We all wished we could report this to CPS, but none of them cared either. They would do nothing about it if a complaint came from us. Even the school didn't seem to object or simply ignored it. However, on one exceptionally cold day, we did notice that Uranus must have driven to the school and taken Tommie used long pants to wear. The school must have called, because Tommie returned home wearing oversized boys pants, probably Grope's – ICK! Katie noticed Tommie's long pants when she met her son at the bus stop. Note something important here. Each day, Katie walked her son to the bus stop and met him coming home. The neighborhood was gang infested. A lot of parents accompanied their kids to/from the bus stop. Therefore, Katie was not stalking anyone like Uranus was claiming to everyone that would listen.

We all wanted to give the children Christmas presents, but we knew that Uranus would simply throw them out. So we held back. We were afraid that Christmas would be miserable for the children. Uranus had told them that they were not getting any Christmas presents from her. She was broke, due to not having a decent job and the cost of the current court case against her. I would have loved to sent grope a can of live bugs to eat (actually a good book) and Tommie a sling shot (with BB's). Oh well, so much for Christmas spirit. However, Curly did send gifts to the kids and these were accepted. I am not sure if the gifts were acknowledged by the kids, however. The church had also contributed something, so Christmas was not a total bust for them.

Me? I had decided way back in October to finally get the hell out of Dodge. My lease was up. Arrowhead was turning ugly and dangerous. Over the summer, the neighborhood had become quite dangerous. I had been accosted by one of the local gang members and had to call the police and have the punk arrested. It turned out that he was one of the leaders and had already been arrested over twenty times. After his arrest I received death threats. They were a nasty bunch of hoods. Store owners were being affected. Business was dropping off. One nearby store was held up at gun point. Parents were getting alarmed and complaining to the Apartment Complex Management staff. Many were moving out, breaking their lease due to criminal harassment. Only Tommie was allowed to go wherever she wanted, Uranus was not there to check on her anyway.

I spent most of my time between Thanksgiving and Christmas packing my belongings. Uranus was pissed off when her precious dirt and endless pots lined the front of her garage. The pile of rotten wood left in my garage was also dumped there. I did spend the time and, with help, carefully moved the contents of her precious crap from my storage areas into her garage one weekend while she was away with Navy boy or someone. I borrowed the key from Nana Anna. Katie and family helped me with relocating her trash collection.

I left New Jersey late in the year (officially January 1st) and moved to a much warmer climate on the deep Southern Coast of North Carolina. I sadly bid farewell to Katie, Cherry, and their families. I said goodbye to New Jersey and hello to hurricanes. Our small friendship group had a farewell dinner at a local restaurant and there was a lot of laughter and some tears. I would miss them all terribly. I intended to stay in touch on a regular basis. I had also promised to finish this novel for their sake as well as my own. Since you are reading it, you know that I kept my promise.

Of course, Uranus rejoiced loudly when I left. She sent email to her military boyfriends stating that she had driven out one of her troublemakers. I did not say goodbye to Tommie and Grope. I had not seen the kids for some time anyway because they were locked in the house except for school, and were under the close eye of Uranus while outside. Uranus avoided me like the plague.

Happy Holidays! I spent Christmas with my daughter and family, and the move went smoothly, thank you very much!

CHAPTER 63
JANUARY-THE CINA CASE ENDS

Would this be the last hearing? We prayed it would be so, but that did not turn out to be the case. Guido had lied to the court. He was still on the case. CPS had complied with the Judges' demands and Tommie had been tested, unfortunately by a low paid and improperly trained Psychologist. It appeared that Uranus was allowed to attend the evaluations and control Tommie's answers; either that or the months of brainwashing had been totally successful. The Psychologist findings were in favor of leaving the children with Uranus; Tommie was "afraid" of Curly and Brady because they were gay. She didn't want to be around queers. Queers were evil.

At the hearing, Guido introduced a number of witnesses on Uranus' behalf, including Grope's teacher Ms. Fargo, the Principal of Grope's school, Booby, and others. The Judge listened with great disinterest to the testimony, and Curly's lawyer Leslie Smart actually made fools of most of them.

Much to the Psychologist's chagrin, she had been subpoenaed to appear and discuss her findings about Tommie. Leslie Smart ripped her to pieces, making her look totally incompetent. It became evident that Tommie was terrified of Uranus, and she said exactly what she thought Uranus wanted her to say. As for the results from the testimony, expectations on Curly's side were high, but Judge Dread, being totally unpredictable, the outcome was a crap shoot. It was mentioned by someone, I believe the Psychologist herself, that Uranus was in far greater need of evaluation than either of the children. Go Figure. Unfortunately, that statement fell upon deaf ears. Was Judge Dread sleeping? HELLO! Judge Dread pondered what he remembered of the statements made during the day, and came to the following finding. The school in Curly's State was just as good if not better than the current school Grope was attending. This was an understatement and one for the good guys, a slap in the face for Uranus – wrong again bitch. Unfortunately, Judge Dread, being the deadbeat that he was, made no other calls, and deferred all the findings of Custody to the Family Court. The fool totally passed the buck. The idiot didn't listen and let the children remain with Uranus "again" for the "time being." He further declared joint custody between Uranus and Curly. I stand corrected. He made two calls, not one. For that Uranus went ballistic again. Then she had the audacity to have Guido ask Judge Dread to allow her to obtain passports for the Children. After strong objections made by Curly, the Judge flatly refused to oblige and deferred that request to family court. As a last gesture, Judge Dread officially closed the CINA case. The inept moron of a Judge had totally blown the case. He should have been dethroned and forced to retire for his actions, but who were we but a bunch of ignorant pawns that had given all we had to help the children. The Judge belonged in a retirement home with full supervision. CPS was totally blown away by it all. All the work they had done, albeit not well done, along with a mountain of evidence against Uranus, was thrown out the window. CASE CLOSED!

CPS was done; Kaput! They were deeply shocked at the outcome and the fact that the Judge did not have the balls to make any real decisions, confirmed their belief that he did not belong in the system. "Judge Dread is a deadbeat, a disgrace to the system, and one of the reasons the system does not work," they said.

Nevertheless, joint custody meant that Uranus no longer had total control of the children. She illustrated her standard demeanor and stormed out of the courtroom, slamming doors as she went. No full custody and no passports. She planned to get even somehow, with everyone.

CHAPTER 64
CHILD PROTECTIVE SERVICES-REALITY SETS IN

At this point in the story, a short essay is appropriate. Child Protective Services - an oxy-moron if there ever was one, at least in Seaford County, is a fact of life. The Seaford County Social Services program consists of a mix of dedicated and some not-so-dedicated, but totally powerless employees, unless a case involves torture, rape, murder, or domestic violence. The State laws and overworked Juvenile Judges tie the hands of the good Social Workers so that, short of a parent molesting or murdering a child, the abusive parent can retain control of the children, especially if the abuser is the mother. The system is unbalanced and pathetic at best. This is especially true because of the terribly flawed political legal system in the State, with ridiculous outdated rules and regulations. Social Services workers are forced to work under the worst of conditions. Blame it on the ACLU? Well, yes in part. Protect the crook and screw the innocent. That's their sick motto. Satin probably runs that organization – at least in my humble opinion.

To be truthful, many Social Workers and Legal Beagles are energetic, but poorly trained to deal with most domestic child abuse and neglect hearings, especially when fighting slimy criminal attorneys like Guido, and facing over-the-hill, burned out, don't-give-a-damn Judges. To make the situation even worse, and I have said this before, most of the Lawyers for the county are contractors and the county is cheap and known to take the low bidder with limited background checks. Of course, in their defense, many of these Lawyers are only given minutes to prepare for court hearings. This is the Counties' fault entirely. That in itself is a travesty of justice.

Folks, this is real life and not like the wonderful show "Judging Amy", now in reruns. Many Juvenile Court Judges, at least in our county, are incompetent, overworked, underpaid and often like the CPS lawyers, are unwilling or unable to spend the time to review cases or the circumstances around them. In their defense, working in a heavy welfare and high crime area, the dockets for these Judges are swamped with abuse and neglect cases and the Judges quickly become burned out or so hardened they just don't give a damn anymore. They collect their paychecks and go play golf. They belong to the same private clubs as slimy lawyers like Guido. They drink their drinks and talk the talk. Screw the kids. They are too busy getting soused to really give a damn about due process. Not all, mind you, but many of them.

Guido knew that he virtually owned Judge Dread, and Judge Dread is only one of the burned out Juvenile Court Judges in Arrowhead. Most Child Protective Services lawyers and Social Workers agree with this consensus. Whatever Guido wanted from this particular Judge, he received more often than not. Move the docket so I get you? OH YEAH, no problem. Let's forget the witnesses, because that would take too long and, besides, it's Miller Time? OK, no sweat. Drop the whole case because it is only about a sick dog. Yep, I agree. Let's go have a drink.

Judge Dread was and remains one of those burned out, disinterested individuals with lots of power, and no real show of concern for the children. He also retains a total disrespect for Social Services, claiming the organization is a total farce and a waste of time. He told this to Guido. Guido told this to me when we were still talking.

Our tiny "support" group, as labeled by CPS, also considered Judge Dread Guido's "pocket Judge." His presence in the system presents a travesty of justice and it hurts only the children, the real victims. He should have retired or moved on years ago or sought out another profession. Tommie and Grope became innocent victims of Judge Dread, placing insane Uranus back in power. I am glad we are through with him.

CHAPTER 65
MORE NEGLECT, MORE DECEIT

T he neglect and brainwashing of the children continued throughout the winter and into the spring. On many occasions in freezing weather, with snow and ice on the ground, Katie saw Tommie standing at the bus stop wearing shorts, while her skinny-assed mother wore warm fur coats, leather boots, and other winter clothing. Grope was nowhere to be seen, of course. He was no longer allowed outside. He preferred to stay in the house in his room naked. We assumed he was still going to school, but he left earlier in the morning and no one went out of their way to check on Uranus or the kids, despite her accusations of stalking.

Regardless of what was observed by our little support group, calling Child Protective Services was no longer an option for any of us. They would not listen to us any longer, and the schools, as far as we could see, did absolutely nothing about the neglect problem.

Spring approached. The whole nightmare has continued for over a year now. I had moved out of state several months back, but kept abreast of the continuing Uranus neglect through Curly and Katie. Cherry had also moved away, expecting her first child. They moved to get away from the dangers in the neighborhood.

Sometimes I lie awake at night and wish I had not started this novel, but I did, and I promised to finish it. As for our efforts in the beginning, we all felt that the welfare of Tommie & Grope was well worth the effort, yet I have now seen and felt the pain the "system" has created for all of us, including the kids, Curly, the Case Workers, and Uranus as well.

The Juvenile Judicial System is so badly flawed and biased toward the neglecting party that the effort we put in now seems futile, but we have already covered that. We were told that Guido finally slipped out of the foreground, and a new lawyer entered the scene for Uranus. I heard that the new lawyer is just as slimy as Guido, but has the advantage of being a practiced Family Lawyer. So far, Uranus appears to have been able to buffalo virtually everyone in the court system, but Guido, being the smart lawyer he is, surely played a large part in her success.

Uranus' lies have continued unchecked. No home visits have been made by CPS since the children were returned to Uranus long ago. Of course Feather, assigned to check up on Uranus and the kids, caused this. Months have passed and Uranus tragically retains residential custody of the children. Her house is totally filthy again. A visit to Uranus' apartment by a friend a couple of weeks ago brought news to Katie that the visitor almost fainted from the smell inside the house. He was not allowed to enter, but just the smell from the partially opened door nearly caused him to vomit. Tommie continues to go to school in shorts, as she did all winter. In other words, everything returned to abnormal.

It is true that joint custody thoroughly enraged Uranus, but she may have found ways around it, or at least developed a new plan. Even with no credit and continued bounced checks, she somehow regained her government clearance. She sent claims to the court to have a job that brings in $4,000 a month. This, of course, was another exaggeration, but no one checked to see if it was true, except us. Unknown to Uranus at that time, she was employed by the same company that Cherry works for. Cherry checked with a friend in personnel and found that Uranus' salary is half of what she claimed to the court. Of course there is still child support and her military disability pay. But $4,000 a month still seems to be a major reach.

Rumors were spread that Uranus may have succeeded in obtaining passports for the children, despite joint custody and the refusal by Curly. Uranus claimed to have a friend at the State Department. If she succeeded in obtaining passports, there is no doubt that she will accept a job overseas as soon as possible, and quickly disappear from everyone's life. But the rumor of passports was probably a fabricated threat tactic on her part.

Maybe it would be best for her to leave the country, but the children would suffer without the support they desperately need from the US school system. Besides, Uranus is delusional in believing that the foreign schools, run by the State Department, are prepared to help special children. I was told that the kids would be tested before going. But then again, Uranus should have been tested before being cleared to go to Iraq. There are so many cracks in the system and Uranus is just slimy enough to slither through most of them.

Our inside "friends" network continues to function and we still have been able to intercept emails sent and received by Uranus to some of her military boyfriends. Uranus gave our friend in the network the keys and never asked for them back, so is that the same as permission to look? Of course, we were not given the emails, only summaries. I have been told that excerpts from her emails state that she blames all of her problems on Katie and me. To her we are evil and insane monsters and are at fault for everything bad that has happened to her, just like the whacko that originally had her arrested because she left the kids home alone. But that is beating a dead horse again.

In one of her emails, Uranus touted complete success in brainwashing her kids into believing that Curly and his gay partner Brady are evil. She expects the kids will refuse to spend part of the summer with them. That is her intent anyway. Uranus and her so-called new lawyer have changed strategy and turned the entire custody process into anti-gay warfare, thinking she can sway the courts into giving her full custody of the children and be granted the withdrawal of any visitation rights from Curly. This, of course, shows her naiveté. The court has already ordered a month of visitation next summer so she will lose this battle. When Grope and Tommie do visit next summer, stay in a real and clean home, enjoy activities, and the love they have never received from Uranus, they should finally realize what a horror their mother really is. Of course, if the kids refuse to go, Uranus will win by default. And that is what she is still working on.

Through Nana Anna, we also have access to summaries of all of her financial transactions. Yep! Nana Anna kept us informed. Uranus still spends like a sailor and bounces checks on a regular basis.

Now all of this inside information I have mentioned here may appear to you as our stalking her. I want to assure you that we are not. We are tracking her lies and deceit and telling no one about it. Most of the data consists of total lies about us, falsehoods about what we are up to, negative statements about our character. We need to protect ourselves. We do not intend to use any of this information against her, but then again, if she enters a lawsuit against us based on these fabricated lies, we need some proof to cover ourselves. You be the judge.

The next, and hopefully final court hearing, is now scheduled and only two weeks away. We are all praying for finality.

CHAPTER 66
HERE COMES THE JUDGE

Finality was just a dream; same type of Judge, different day. Uranus appeared in court without her "new and awesome" lawyer. The lawyer was a cover, a lie of course. Curly misunderstood what the hearing was all about, thought he was not required, so he did not appear. This was nearly a fatal mistake at this point, and in the long run it was. Curly's lawyer did show up to court, declaring that she is closing her business, moving to another state, and formally withdrawing from the case. Curly would need a new lawyer if he decided to continue. Leslie Smart seemed to have forgotten that she told Curly that he was not needed at the hearing; that his attendance was an option. This was her mistake, not Curly's.

As stated before, the Psychologist had told Judge Dread that both children wanted to stay with mom. The children said the same thing to the Family Court Judge. Again, injustice prevailed, and the Judge let the kids remain with Uranus for now. Of course the kids wanted to stay with mom. The witch had brainwashed them for months on end. Let's get real here folks. The Judge was just plain afraid of committing to anything, and the Psychologist was totally inept. The operational words are "mom does prevail," regardless of her mental state. The fact that Leslie Smart obliterated the Psychologists' weak testimony was not even read or brought up. Had the Judge read any of the transcripts? It was doubtful at best.

At that point in the hearing Uranus smelled a total victory coming and demanded full custody of the children, passports for the children, and the case to be completely dropped. Thank God the Judge had some sense and denied the requests. See, the passport statement was another ruse. The Judge set another hearing for June. So Uranus did get what she wanted, at least a part. Another delay meant more of a chance to get rid of Curly. But joint custody remained in place, and still no passports.

Uranus was absolutely livid about the denial of passports and the remaining joint custody. Once again, she put on a show, storming out of the courtroom. Sound like a broken record? You bet!

She continued her lies by writing emails to all of her friends informing them that Curly didn't pay his lawyer and the lawyer dropped him like a rock. She said the case was going to go in her favor. She claimed Curly was a coward and was finally showing his true colors. She also mentioned that Guido is still with her, acting in the background, and he will put the squeeze on the court to nail Curly for more money. Yes, Guido came up with the deception. Uranus closed her email by saying that there would be one last hearing in June and the nightmare would finally be over. The "evil ones" who started all this would be out of the picture and helpless to do anything.

CHAPTER 67
WHO HAS GAS?

Months passed. All of us were hurt; badly hurt. We had talked to Curly. We explained to him that Uranus bragged in her emails to her buddies that she had successfully brainwashed the children and they were now totally alienated from their father. They did not want to talk with him or see him ever again. Curly was terribly hurt. Yes, Uranus had done her evil work very well.

June and the final appearing date approached. Youth gangs continued to be a problem in the local area. In late May, Tommie was outside in the parking lot near Katie's complex. She was being pushed around by some neighborhood thugs. Katie spotted this and ran the kids off. I told her in a later phone call that she was brave to do this but be careful. "These kids carry weapons," I said. After running off the bullies, Katie asked Tommie if she was OK. Tommie looked very sad but said yes, so Katie turned and started back toward her apartment. Tommie hesitated. Katie looked back. It became evident to Katie that Tommie wanted her to stay with her. After all, the punks might return. So she turned around, walked back, and remained with her for a while, comforting Tommie as best she could.

At that time another big break came. At long last, Tommie started to open up again and talk. For some time, at a distance, it had seemed clear to Katie that Tommie needed to talk to someone, but Tommie remained terrified that her mom would find out. Tommie was still in lockdown, forbidden to speak to anyone, or even play outside after school. Today, Tommie had escaped outside for a break from being tormented by Grope. If mom wasn't home, what harm could it do?

We all know and appreciate that Tommie loves animals. Before her lockdown, Tommie used to walk neighborhood dogs for a little money. Tommie told Katie that Mom had encouraged Tommie to breed and raise rats in their apartment. There were babies now. Tommie also had an advanced case of ringworm on her arm and showed it to Katie. The ringed wound was large, ugly, untreated and oozing. Uranus blamed that on a stray cat Tommie had touched. However, she did not treat the infection and told Tommie to continue to go to school, knowing full well that ringworm is contagious. Well, let's give her the benefit of doubt and say that she didn't know. Uranus is very stupid in many ways. Regardless, the infection should have been treated and the school should have known and sent her home. Later, we all joked that Tommie probably caught the infection from Grope or mom. In reality though, Uranus was probably right. The ringworm was probably transmitted to Tommie by the stray cat, because cats are natural ringworm carriers – a little trivia I am sure you will enjoy. Have cats?

We had heard from neighbors with kids that had visited Tommie a short time ago that her apartment was again a sewer; the rats were allowed to run free in the apartment, feces were everywhere. Sadly, for Tommie, one of the rats died after chewing up the inside of the dishwasher trying to get out. How it got in there no one will ever know. Could it be ... Grope?

Feeling sad and not knowing what else to do, Tommie told Katie that she placed the dead and partly decomposed rat in a plastic bag and "buried" it in the refrigerator, where it remained as of this conversation. Yep! Uranus was rarely home and the kids were neglected and living in total filth again. Of course,

Child Protective Services had not made a single visit to the home after the kids were taken the summer before. Feather, we were positive, had made sure Uranus was not bothered again. They were still buddies. Now the CINA case closed, so no visits would be conducted.

Tommie then told Katie that mom did not come home until very late at night. According to mom, this was because of work. Tommie knew this was a lie and said so. Navy boy was history, having found a real girlfriend. Uranus had a new boyfriend she was coupling with and often did not get home until nearly midnight.

Tommie announced to Katie that they had no hot water in the house and literally no food to eat. The gas had been off for a long time now. We later learned from a local friend working for the Gas Company that the gas bill had not been paid since last August, nearly a year ago. The amount due was huge, nearly $1,500.00. We suspect that the gas company waited until deep winter was past because of the children and then turned the gas off.

Katie asked about Grope. Tommie said that he was now terrified of the light and did not want to go outside, but forced himself to go to school. How much truth there was in that was questionable. Maybe Grope was morphing into a night crawler, but that did not seem realistic. Tommie said that Grope was also afraid to ride in the car and no longer went anywhere with them. This may be true because Uranus always forced him, a big kid now, to sit in the cramped back seat that was always loaded with junk and smelly. Bottom line, we concluded that Grope's condition had probably worsened. Uranus was destroying him completely. But then again, Tommie was learning to be a really good fibber.

Katie told me during a phone call some days later that she could not let the discussion with Tommie pass unreported, and had notified Child Protective Services once again. What else could she do? I told her that it was her responsibility to do so, having heard a cry for help from Tommie. Uranus had once again shown that she is the monster of all mothers - or is it mother of all monsters? When Katie called, CPS took notes once again, or said they did, and indicated immediate interest in the situation. The Social Worker stated that they would follow up and get back to her. Katie was called back and told by Selma that CPS had been waiting to pounce on Uranus, knowing that there would be another report forthcoming at some point. Yeah right!

Katie and I discussed the gas matter further. I suspected that no hot water meant that they had no electricity, as well. She said that no one had seen lights in the apartment for a long time but she would check into it. That turned out to not be the case – at this point. That came later. However, at this time, the gas range was covered with cardboard and cooking was done with a tiny hot plate. We learned this from Nana Anna, who happened to go back to the apartment to collect what was left of her stuff before she moved out of town. Yes, she was finally moving on and out of the area. Uranus would never pay her back what she owed her, and Nana Anna would not take Uranus to court.

Complaining to the Apartment Manager once again was out of the question because Uranus owned her. Furthermore, our concern about CPS was that we had heard so many promises before without any real results. Would things change? It was doubtful.

Selma called Katie again a few days later and told her that Uranus had explained to them that the gas had only been off for a day or two for tests by the gas company. She said that there was a gas problem in the house. Of course this was a total lie. But the lie worked, and CPS took the bait. The supervisor at CPS decided not to open a case, giving Uranus complete benefit of doubt.

I was totally outraged at the news. I suggested that we find backup about the neglect during the winter and that there were probably several individuals that could come to support us. Katie would look into this. She did and found support.

I said that I would write a factual letter to the Director of Health and Human Services for Seaford County and file a formal complaint, threatening to call in the papers and TV stations unless an investigation was opened. We had to nail her wicked, lying ass to the concrete. This may be our last shot.

CHAPTER 68
DEAR DIRECTOR

September 1

Ms. Petunia W. Conklin, Director
Department of Health and Human Services
401 Haggard Drive
Arrowhead NJ

Dear Ms. Conklin;

I am deeply concerned about the welfare of two children that reside at the Maytag Apartments in Arrowhead New Jersey. You are most likely familiar with the case involving Tommie and Grope and their neglectful mother Uranus. If you are not familiar, you should be.

I was the individual that initially reported the neglect mid last year, which continues even today on a daily basis. I also appeared in court on your behalf in an attempt to remove the children from the home and send them home with their father, Curly, who wants them and is quite capable of taking care of them.

Their mother, Uranus, has been totally successful in lying her way through the system, using a very smart, ill reputed criminal lawyer to help her twist the facts and make your Social Services Department look foolish.

After the children were returned home by the court; on the single occasion we know of when a visit to Uranus' premise actually took place, Mom was given plenty of advance notice prior to the visit, allowing her to "cover up" all of the serious health hazards that would have guaranteed removal of the children.

Here are some recent facts. There are several witnesses who will back this up.

- *Tommie was encouraged by mom to breed rats. These rodents have reproduced and are given freedom to run about the house. Mom does not clean up after them.*
- *Tommie suffers from Ringworm that appears on her left arm. This infection was unchecked for weeks and no appointment was made for her to see a doctor, nor did she do anything about it. Tommie also stated to a neighbor that she also has it on her feet. She has had this infection for several weeks and mom has done little, if anything about it. Tommie was told to go to school with full knowledge that the virus is infectious. The school neglected to do anything about it.*
- *Tommie was sent to school throughout much of the winter in shorts, even though mom was dressed in heavy, warm clothing. She was observed by many neighbors at the school bus stop in shorts, even on icy and snow days. The school neglected to do anything about it. This is blatant neglect.*
- *Tommie plays outside when her mother is not at home. This is the only time caring neighbors are able to talk with her. She has recently opened up about many things which are quite disturbing. These are statements Tommie has recently made.*
- *Tommie stated that quite some time ago the gas was turned off and the children have taken cold showers. That does not promote good hygiene. Tommie stated today that she likes cold showers. I think a check with the gas company will confirm that the gas has been off for a considerable period of time.*
- *Uranus' Foster mother Nana Anna was in the apartment a couple of days ago and told us that the gas is still off and that cooking has been done with a hot plate. Uranus does not allow paper plates or plastic utensils in the house; therefore, the dishes must be unsanitary. The range was covered with cardboard – a fire hazard if and when the gas is turned on.*
- *Grope does not go outside ever and stays in his room. This is unhealthy; more so because of his autism. He is hygienically unclean. Tommie also stated that Grope is*

afraid to ride in a car now. Uranus and Tommie go out, while Grope remains at home alone.

- *Uranus often stays out at night, not returning until very late at night. Mom claims this is work, but Tommie knows this is not true. During this time the kids go without food. Is there food in the house? Are the kids cooking with the hot plate?*
- *Tommie is chronically late to school. The school has done nothing about this. WHY? Tommie is not supervised at all by mom. School and homework are Tommie's responsibility and if she elects to screw up – that's her own fault. Uranus does not set a bed time, wake her in the morning, prepare breakfast, or see her off to school. Uranus does not check her homework or participate with her studies. Uranus is not home to supervise her. Both children remain unsupervised. There is no babysitter other than Tommie.*

Now what promotes neglect? I quote from The County's Web Page.

"WHAT IS CHILD ABUSE AND NEGLECT?

NEGLECT: Child neglect is the chronic failure of a parent, caretaker, household or family member to provide a child under 18 with basic needs of life, such as: food, clothing, shelter, medical care, attention to hygiene, educational opportunity, protection, and supervision."

Mom, on a regular basis violates all of these items except a roof over her head.

WHAT CONSTITUTES REPORTING NEGLECT?

Again I quote from the County's Web Page:

"WHEN AND HOW DO I REPORT SUSPECTED CHILD ABUSE AND NEGLECT?

A report should be made when there is reason to SUSPECT that a child or adolescent has been abused or neglected. A report of suspected child abuse is only a request for an investigation. The person making the report does not need to prove the abuse or neglect. Investigation and determination of results are the responsibility of Child Protection Service workers and the police. A person may make an anonymous report. If a report of child abuse or neglect is made "in good faith," the reporting source is immune from both civil and criminal liability.

REMEMBER: The person making the report does not need to prove the abuse or the neglect."

In summary, it is obvious and the case history verified this, Uranus has continuously neglected her children, one of which is a special needs child. You folks were unsuccessful last time. This is a FORMAL report of neglect. I know the history. I insist that you follow up this time and do it right. New reports and calls have been made to your department by the father and another concerned neighbor. I have heard that you are not opening a case. I insist as a citizen that you do. These children are at risk. I firmly believe that Uranus is a pathological liar and seriously neglectful. She has psychologically damaged the children into believing whatever she wants them to believe. Uranus has claimed that she is being persecuted, stalked, and lied about because of spite. This could not be further from the truth. We, as caring neighbors, spent over a year trying to see that the children wound up protected and well taken care of. They are entitled to that. The father wants them and can care for them. Curly is willing to take them but cannot afford to be continually jerked around by the system and forced leave work and travel thousands of miles over and over again because of planned delays by Uranus , an inept Judge, and a slimy lawyer.

Lastly, I ask that you please do NOT use Feather to check into this because I firmly believe she is biased. I like Feather but believe Uranus has her under her thumb. I ask that you follow up and speak with Ms Selma and the Attorneys that have prosecuted the case more than once for in depth history. The last year has been torture on the kids and all of us that honestly care for them.

I recently moved out of state, but visit often and check in regularly with neighbors and friends. I know first hand that the abuse continues. If you have questions, you can reach me at 555 246-5555.

NOTE: This email is confidential and is not to be disclosed to ANYONE outside your direct organization. Last time, my name was leaked to Uranus' lawyer Guido. I was told he got it from your office. I paid a terrible price.

Thank you for your help and immediate attention to this mater. Please advise me that you have opened a case and followed up. That is all I need to know. I ask for nothing else. If I do not hear back, I will consider forwarding this letter and other provable facts to the State Attorney's office, ABC, CBS, NBC, and request immediate action.

Sincerely, CJ Kingsley
5877 Coastal Hwy
Surf City, North Carolina

I had prepared a letter for Congress and the news, but was pleased to hear back from the Chief Case Evaluator from the Director's Office that the review of my letter did indeed justify a case being opened and one had been. Hope remains eternal.

CHAPTER 69
HERE COMES THE JUDGE

June arrived and the planned custody hearing was held. Much to the chagrin of Uranus, nothing much happened, and yet another hearing was scheduled for sometime in August. It has been a year since Uranus returned from Iraq. We would like to believe the hearing delay was requested by the investigation by Health and Human Services. Curly was informed and it appears the he is still in the picture somewhere. Uranus, of course, still believes that all of the problems will go away and she can get on with her neglectful life without interference. With a little help from above, Uranus may see the kiss of death (to her anyway) with the children being removed from her evil clutches. Again, this sounds like a broken record: "only time will tell."

CHAPTER 70
SUMMER SCHOOL AND THE SCOOTER

Now that July set in and the temperatures ranged in the low 100s, I would have liked to say that life settled down for Tommie, but it hadn't.

If you remember the incident last year when Tommie was caught walking home from school – while Uranus was in Iraq. One would think that lessons had been learned at that time. The grade school was remiss in reporting the incident to Child Protective Services back then and it became totally apparent that Uranus had the entire school staff buffaloed. The only person threatened at the time was Nana Anna.

We know that Tommie transferred schools in the fall of last year, entering seventh grade. The new school is nearly two miles away from her apartment, if you can call it that. We know that during the entire winter months the poor child wore shorts to school and we figured that the schools had done nothing about it. Was the new school under the evil spell of Uranus, believing every word she said? Winter turned to spring and we recall that Uranus had not paid the gas bill since last August so it was finally turned off in March or early April because of her huge debt. Now shorts in the freezing weather turned into cold showers and the use of a dangerous hot plate for cooking.

Recall that I wrote a letter to the Director of Health and Human Services in the spring and received a response from them that Uranus was once again under formal investigation. By now you would think that the pathetic woman would have learned to be a little more careful with her neglect. WRONG! Any psychiatrist will tell you after analyzing Uranus that she has a serious problem with any type of authority, a socio-pathological resistance to authority of any kind. Here is another example of her absolute defiance of the law. I know, another broken record. What can I say?

Tommie failed seventh grade and was forced to attend summer school. Uranus makes it a point to take Tommie to school on her way to work each morning, which makes Tommie late to school every day, otherwise it would interfere with her private schedule. Last Tuesday the weather turned dangerously hot, over 100 degrees, and the air quality index was announced as code red, stay inside. Katie picked her son up from summer school and spotted Tommie riding her scooter home from school. Katie, knowing how dangerous it was outside, not even considering the danger of the local gangs, pulled over and asked Tommie if she would like a ride home and Tommie replied: "I can't. I am not allowed." Katie went home and checked the State law once more. The distance is too far. It is illegal for Tommie to walk or ride a scooter home from school. There is also a summer school bus available for her to take from school that stops close to home, but she refuses to take it. So Katie called the school and reported the incident. The receptionist asked if Tommie was still on the school grounds – Duh! The receptionist said there was nothing she could do about it. In a bit of a rage, Katie demanded to speak with the school counselor.

Mr. Radcliff picked up the call and a long discussion began. Katie did not even need to tell him her name or the name of the student involved. He knew. Katie said that she was not out to get anyone in trouble, but she was a neighbor, cared for the girl and was concerned, not only because of the heat, but because the area had become gang infested. She was worried Tommie might be in danger because she was attacked before. The counselor responded with news that set Katie back a bit. First of all, Mr. Radcliff said that he had seen Tommie off the grounds just after school on her scooter on her way somewhere. He also reported that Uranus was under investigation by Child Protective Services and that he, himself, had reported Tommie and Uranus to CPS on a number of occasions. He knew the gas had been turned off and, for all he knew, it still was. He said he could say no more, but promised to talk to Tommie the very next day and report the incident to CPS.

Of course, Katie called me immediately with the news. I am so relieved that the school has at last become involved. They have admitted that they are aware of the neglect and have been working with CPS. However, here is the dilemma. Why are the children still with the mother? Everyone, it seems, is fully aware of what the woman is and the neglect that continues on a daily basis. It still seems to me that the system is totally broken down. Recall, folks that I quoted the law in my letter to the County and gave proof of Uranus' breaking virtually every law but one – a roof over their heads, filthy and stinky, but a roof. Where is the root of the problem? The system is corrupt and ineffective.

So the investigation is in progress. How much can we believe? I am not sure. We can just pray that we are being given the truth and some type of action is taking place. I have been at this for a year and a half now and want to finish this novel at some point in my life. So the saga continues and chapters keep rolling out that report the horrors and lack of action as they occur. (i.e., broken records)

There is one more thing to report to you readers today, since this has now becoming more of a diary of evil events. Curly was informed about the latest issues and called CPS. He offered to come pick up the children, but he would only fly there, tickets in hand, if he could take them home for good. So Curly is still a hero in my heart.

Dear readers, does this sound trivial? There is no more comedy here. There is a beautiful twelve year-old child that is being taught to lie and break the law. She runs loose in a dangerous neighborhood and will be accosted at some point. The gangs are real – both male and female. The neighborhoods are just not safe anymore.

I feel for Tommie because this is virtually her only time outside being free. Why? Mom does not allow her outside the apartment at anytime without her being present. Uranus is afraid that Tommie will talk to someone – and justifiably so. Mom would get speared.

Then there is also a fourteen, almost fifteen, year old Autistic Child that is brilliant in many ways but completely socially retarded. His life will be ruined if he does not get help. When will this tragedy end?

CHAPTER 71
AUGUST 2-FINAL FAMILY COURT HEARING

The day before the hearing, Uranus forced Tommie to try on girls clothes borrowed from a neighbor, since she didn't have anything but boy clothes in her small, worn out and dirty wardrobe. Tommie was repulsed at the idea of wearing a dress, but went along with it for the hearing. The clothes even smelled clean, which for Tommie was not comfortable. Grope was happy to dress up and sat there silent and drooling, with his bionnacle stuffed into his left paw. Both children had been so severely brainwashed by now that there was no doubt what they would say to the Judge in court.

Curly had offered, but now had given up and decided to not show up to court again. There would just be more delays. Uranus would find a way. Sometimes, evil wins over good. At long last Uranus was in her element, she stated this in emails to her friends after the hearing. Uranus had long prepared for this day, still believing that any money from Curly had come from garnished wages and claimed the Judge took it hook line and sinker. Curly was labeled as an unfit father. Lies, lies, and more lies flowed like poisoned honey off her snake-like tongue. Paranoia, Schizophrenia, and Pathological lies prevail even in the best of times. And on this day the Judge took the bait and swallowed it along with the hook. He awarded Uranus full and permanent custody of the children. Any future visitation by the father was to be at Uranus' discretion – which would never happen unless Curly was willing to go to court on his own. She had won – big time. Her lies and distorted facts, using advice from her slimy lawyer Guido, had paid off at long last.

Fortunately for her, she did not need to show any of her prepared material in court. That would have opened up her brain like a can of rotten worms.

The evening after the hearing, Uranus wrote to friends and said that she could finally get those passports for the kids and take them on an exotic vacation in Thailand, Cambodia, and Viet Nam when she had the money. They would go maybe as early as next year. This would be interesting, since she still had no gas, the bill unpaid for a year and the fact that her car was soon to be impounded for suspended tags again, and the electricity was now off.

CHAPTER 72
VENGEANCE IS MINE SAYETH THE BITCH

Vengeance would finally be hers, thought Uranus. She had tried last week in court to file a protective restraining order against Katie, but failed, due to absolutely no evidence. After the final hearing, she called CPS and talked to the Supervisor asking her to mark Katie as one that files false reports. The supervisor agreed to check into it. Of course, that failed too. All of Katie's calls were legitimate and they had evidence to back them up. Little did Uranus know that the new case against her was still open, but who knows what would ever happen. CPS was tired of dealing with her and like Curly, prepared to give up. Their case backlog of child abuse was just too large. Uranus began bragging to her friends that the Orwellian Nazi's, her name for the Child Protective Services Organization, had been put in their place and would be further embarrassed by Guido through a nasty letter he was writing. Of course, that letter never came. Uranus was delusional again.

Months later, Uranus told a friend that she and Guido were going to formally sue CPS for illegally taking her children and placing her son in an institution without consulting his school, plus accusing her of neglect based on false reports and fake email. This statement sounded exactly like desperate Uranus, using whatever means she could to get even, possibly making a lot of money. All of us believe that the lawsuit, if Guido was foolish enough to file one, would be laughed out of court, because her accusations were totally baseless.

We are also convinced that Uranus will screw up again, but we are through with her, CPS and the Court system. We have done all we can do within the law. To us, Uranus is history and the kids are lost forever.

CHAPTER 73
THE RUSE CONTINUES

More time passed. Nothing was done about the new investigation, as we expected. Uranus had lied to the court so many times that further impostures were of no big consequence to her, in fact within her pathetic mind she believed what she said to the Court and to CPS to be true. The electricity was turned back on a few weeks later. The Gas remained off well into the fall, until cold showers were no longer refreshing; until cold showers became unbearable. She finally took money from her monthly rent and paid the Gas Company $500 so they would once again have heat. Of course that very month, she blew hundreds of dollars on DVD movies and other non-essentials. Her spendthrift habits continued, with other bills unpaid.

According to Nana Anna, Uranus spent nearly three hundred dollars on haircuts for her and Tommie. Tommie got a Mohawk because her mom had one at her age. Sadly, the kids at school began teasing her, calling her a lesbian, homo, freak, and other horrible names. Tommie began wearing a ball cap to hide her head.

When I heard of this, I drove to New Jersey just to see her. Well I wanted to see her, but had actually planned the trip to see Katie. I waited for Tommie at her school bus stop, waited for her to step off her bus. Seeing her after so long a time almost brought tears to my eyes. It was true, her beautiful hair was gone and she looked rather like a shaved raccoon with bald sides and long hair topping the crown of her head, forming into a long tail that hung down her back below her shoulder blades. That look and the oversized black rimmed glasses that sat on her tiny nose perfected the image. She was first off the bus. She stopped dead in her tracks and almost bolted the other way when she saw me, but after a few moments she gathered her courage and walked by me, looking at me out of the sides of her eyes.

I said softly looking right at her, "Hello Tommie."

She replied in a whisper, "hello."

"How are you," I asked?

Again, another whisper from her as she finally glanced at me; "Fine."

I couldn't bear doing this. I missed her so much and felt so badly for her, but knew it best that I leave her alone. I simply said, "Tommie, it is very nice to see you once again. Bye." I left her and I walked across the street to catch up with Katie's son and to meet with Katie. She had observed the whole thing.

Talking to Katie about thirty yards away, I saw that Tommie stood at the corner for a long time talking with her friend; she kept looking over at me almost as if wanting me to come back. Previously, this is how Tommie alerted us that she wanted to talk. I resisted the urge and decided to keep my distance – a wise choice.

Later that evening Cherry and her beautiful new baby drove to Katie's house and we all met and walked down the street to have dinner together. Cherry had seen Tommie while driving in and stopped to talk to her. I learned from Cherry later that evening at dinner that Tommie's seeing me freaked her out. Uranus had told Tommie that it was just a "troublemakers" reunion, and that I was only visiting. It hurt to know that Uranus had successfully programmed Tommie and Grope to fear me. I would never have hurt them. I only wanted what was best for them and that was to get them away from the psychotic witch. But I had mellowed over time and knew why Uranus was afraid of me. She felt threatened and knew I wielded the truth, and she carried nothing but a bag full of lies. I drove home the following day, thinking how pathetic Uranus really is and wishing for a miracle to help the children. We all knew the Court System and CPS had failed, and weren't going to ever help them.

CHAPTER 74
BAIL OUT

Katie called me at home in North Carolina and told me that Uranus had been notified that she must pay the rent on time and find a new co-signer on the lease, otherwise vacate the apartment. It wouldn't be long before Uranus and her children would be on the street. "She is broke and has no place to go. The hammer is about to fall," Katie said.

Shortly thereafter, late in the evening after the office had closed, a big moving truck showed up. Uranus and a new male "friend" packed the truck and drove off in the early hours of the morning. Uranus left the apartment a filthy, infested mess. It cost the Company thousands of dollars to repair the damage, including the water damage caused by her illegal water bed. The Maytag Managers had been warned long ago that she was a flight risk, so it was their own fault. Building Management tried to sue her, but failed because she left no forwarding address. The kids did not report to school. Uranus had simply vanished.

CHAPTER 75
EPILOGUE

"A mistake which is commonly made about neurotics is to suppose that they are interesting. It is not interesting to be always unhappy, engrossing with oneself, malignant and ungrateful, and never quite in touch with reality."

- Cyril Connoly

We finally reach the end of this story. I am sure all of you readers that stuck with me and read the entire book are anxious to know what happened to everyone involved – at least over the past few years. If you skipped to the end, you missed all of the good stuff.

Uranus finally lost the children. How she lost them is quite interesting. It had nothing to do with CPS or a fair Juvenile Court System. The children finally realized their mother was totally insane. Uranus had found a friend to stay with temporarily, hidden from everyone. Tommie filed a petition through the courts for both herself and her brother, Grope, to be allowed to live with their father, Curly. Tommie filed, and Grope went along with her. He was too out of it to really make any type of decision on his own. Having received the subpoena, Uranus went postal, but the children had been taken during school for protection and remained adamant. They were placed together in Foster care temporarily until the hearing was finalized. Because they were old enough to choose, Uranus had no more control. She fought bitterly, went into a rage in court, and had to be removed from the room by force. Curly and Brady flew in for the hearing and stated to the judge that they were happy to take them in.

After losing the children to Curly, crying for about ten minutes, Uranus packed up her treasures – at least the ones she hadn't hocked, reinstated herself with KBR and moved back to Iraq. All this happened within weeks. KBR never did give her a Psych exam. What a mistake!

She stayed in Camp Fallujah for a couple of years or so, earning lots of bucks. Uranus actually saved quite a bit of money, having paid no taxes, and successfully avoided child support payments. Uranus never contacted her kids again, dismissing them as losers. She became totally content with her own warped life.

Tommie and Grope quickly forgot about Uranus' existence – which was a blessing. I heard from a Marine Officer friend stationed in Fallujah that Uranus was just starting her third year on the job when she was caught on base in the middle of a threesome in the back of a medical truck. It wouldn't have been so bad, except for the fact that the threesome consisted of two young Marines, namely the Base Commanders twin son and daughter. To make it worse, she gave both of the kids the clap. Uranus was fired on the spot and sent back to the States where she somehow jointly purchased and reopened the Mustang Ranch in Nevada. Word on the street is that she has been quite successful – go figure.

Stepping back a bit, Curly had been called by the court and he agreed to full and unconditional custody of the kids. The hearing was fast and simple. Curly and Brady took the children home with them and within a short time the kids became the happiest they had ever been. It took a lot of work, but the kids really came around. Curly and Brady are very proud of their progress. Over the next several years, Curly lost his hair raising Grope, but that is understandable considering the number of brain sucking sessions he had to endure before Grope evolved into a human. Now Curly matches Brady – twin chrome domes. Brady is Grope's true Entomologist buddy, except that he won't eat bugs.

Nana Anna moved away for a while and she is now home with her original family. Unfortunately, her mother died before she moved back, but she did get to visit with her a few times. Nana Anna visits with Curly and the children often, content never to hear from Uranus again. She was never paid back the money Uranus owed to her – no big surprise there.

Grope, after much intense therapy, vastly improved his social behavior. He has grown up a lot and traded the Bionnacle collection for a quality fishing pole. Often times he can be seen on the front pond of his Dad's property or at the local lake, popping a couple of wiggly worms or crickets in his mouth while he baits the hook. Surprisingly, he can still read in the dark. Well, not so surprising, since he still eats bugs. He also has been rated as a genius in Math and Biological Sciences in the excellent special school he attends. He actually has some friends now and that is great news.

Tommie is a straight "A" student and in senior High School. She is also a Varsity cheerleader. Once in a while her front tooth falls out while doing a flip or two and everyone chuckles, but that's OK because her hair grew back in long and beautiful and she developed into the prettiest and most popular girl in school. Unlike her mom, she developed a nice figure and boobs – just as it should be.

Katie's husband Jack retired from the Navy after twenty years. They moved the family back home to PA, where they now live quite happily raising their kids. We remain friends and have stayed in contact over the years, visiting once in a while during the summer months.

Cherry and her husband, Martin, built their big house in the country, and also purchased a small tennis club which was always her husband's dream. Turning the business was a lot of work. I hear that they are doing nicely and are quite happy. I also understand that they are currently out shopping for diapers and such for a brand new baby – number three I believe.

As for me, I am the same – just a little older. The only excitement is that I am currently in the middle of a big liable lawsuit involving my latest published essay, in which I clearly define the ineptitude of the Seaford County Social Services Division, Judicial System, and Lawmakers. I guess I pissed off a Senator and Congressman or two. That's OK though, because I hired Guido and he is kicking butt. I am proud to say that Judge Dread has the case, since he moved to Civil Court. Yep. It takes a crook to beat a crook they say – sometimes more than one.

POST-MORTEM

Before sending this work to my Publisher, my editor and I spent quite a bit of time reading and editing the book, applying finishing touches here and there. I found that many chapters demonstrated a vindictive tone and I felt some shame in showing my emotion, anger, and frustration to you readers. I guess we all want revenge at times.

One dear friend of mine, part of my test reader group, read the book before it was published. She said that she laughed a lot, but was chilled by the many gross events that took place. In the end, my friend said that I went a bit far with spiteful text toward the mother and the system. My friend also said that any mother (most anyway) will fight for her children and do whatever it takes to keep them safe; in other words, they will lie, cheat, steal, and even commit murder. Defense Lawyers will almost do the same.

My immediate rebuttal was strong although my friend made a very good point. You read all of my rebuttal points in the novel. How many mothers let their young daughter go to school in 15 degree weather in shorts – at least four days a week? How many mothers throw out perfectly good warm clothes because a woman she hates bought them for the kids with the little money she had? How many mothers spend child support checks on themselves only and let the children go without? How many mothers tell their children that they will receive no help on their homework – they are on their own – period? How many mothers allow a daughter to wander around a gang infested neighborhood at all hours? How many mothers teach their children to lie; in fact, encourage lies if they or she can benefit from them? How many mothers bring in boyfriends on their first date and sleep with them – keep the kids and neighbors awake with erotic noise? Worse, how many mothers leave their young children alone at home while she is out with anyone that will give her pleasure (in my characters case only military, police or firemen – heroes, men in uniform)? Don't forget that one of the Children has Asperger's Syndrome and requires continuous supervision. What about the possibility of sexual abuse? How many mothers let their children live in absolute filth, including allowing pet rats to run free in the house? How many mothers spend money on themselves, rather than paying the utility bills, resulting in the gas and electricity being turned off for months at a time? How many mothers do not tell their kids she loves them? Perhaps there are too many. Perhaps I live in a closet. I am sure that there are just as many neglectful men in the world. But I personally feel that mentally ill, neglectful sluts like Uranus deserve to lose their children, especially when someone is willing and able to give them proper care and love. Sexual preferences of the parent or guardian should be moot. Gays make good parents too. Remember, there is usually a lot of truth in fiction. Sometimes there is more truth than in non-fiction because the writer can take liberties not normally taken.

My past wife, God rest her soul, was in many ways an Irish saint during our 34 years of marriage. She took in many stray children. The door was always open and these children never went without – especially in the food, clothing, health, love and guidance departments. We even fostered a child, but mostly just took them in off the streets when asked by their parents or when they had no place to go. Most of the kids that lived with us turned out to be outstanding individuals. Yes, we had a failure or two, but we did our best and most of the kids turned out great. So perhaps I am bitter because I have seen the good side of hard.

I am quite bitter about the inept legal and child protective system in our county, and feel the system is more political than conscientious. Don't get me wrong. There are a lot of great and caring Social Workers, Lawyers and Judges out there. If this book does anything for those that read it, I hope it teaches the reader to hug their kids and tell them you love them every day, carefully manage their lives, and spend the time to guide them into becoming happy and productive adults. It is also important for people to look out for others not so caring and to not be afraid to report what appears to be neglect or abuse. The system may be cracked or broken, but it does work sometimes. You need to try. Take the leap. Lastly, please be outspoken and vote to improve the child protection laws and the Juvenile Court System in general. Children's lives are at stake here. Children are the future of our wonderful, but imperfect, country. What we do now matters. I pray this book makes you think about these things.

THE END

Printed in the United States
96361LV00003B/207/A